Endorsements

"The greatest teacher about life I know of is death. For decades, I have watched people heal their lives when they were forced to accept their mortality. Sharon Lund's experience and wisdom can help you to heal, free yourself from fear and truly live in the time of your life. Read and learn the lessons we are all here to learn. Become a student of life through Sharon's instructions."

Bernie Siegel, M.D.
Author of *Help Me to Heal* and
101 Exercises for the Soul

"Reverend Sharon Lund has created a unique jewel of a book that honors both the sanctity of life and the sacredness of death. Her practical suggestions for creating a "Legacy of Love" capture the essence of what it means to be truly human."

Joan Borysenko, Ph.D.
Author of
Minding the Body, Mending the Mind, and
Your Soul's Compass: What is Spiritual Guidance?

"Sacred Living, Sacred Dying *honors and celebrates everyone's most holy and inevitable journey — while heartfully preparing its readers for the ultimate and meaningful questions and reflections concerning the living dance of death.*"

Dr. John F. Demartini
Author of *Count Your Blessings —*
The Healing Power of Gratitude and Love

"*This exceptional book demonstrates the personal impact each of us has on the lives of those we touch whether they are personal friends, patients, or casual acquaintances. The many creative suggestions are a valuable resource and assist us in thinking outside the box of our day-to-day chaplaincy.*"

Christian Richard Demlow, DMin BCC

"Sacred Living, Sacred Dying *is the breakthrough book that shows exactly what it means to leave a legacy of love.*"

Ken Druck. Ph.D.
Founder, The Jenna Druck Foundation
Families Helping Families

"Sharon Lund's Sacred Living, Sacred Dying: A Guide to Embracing Life and Death *is a "must" book for anyone who cares about their loved ones. This creative and unique piece of work epitomizes the personal impact we each have on our friends and family and how important we are to them in life and in death. The many ideas and creative suggestions are a tribute to the importance of the human spirit in life and a sacred physical death in these masterfully created pages."*

> Jack E. Stephens, J.D., LL.M.,
> Estate Planning Attorney

"Sacred Living, Sacred Dying *is beneficial for the healthiest, or those faced with a terminal illness, as a special way to have their memories live on after their transition."*

> Greg Hahn, R.N.
> Director of Client Services
> LightBridge Hospice

Sacred Living, Sacred Dying

Sacred Living, Sacred Dying

A Guide to Embracing Life and Death

To Agnes —
You have wisdom
and precious memories
that will be appreciated
for generations. Enjoy
your journey.
Love & Blessings.
Sharon

Sharon Lund

Foreword by Stephen and Ondrea Levine

Sacred Life Publishers™
www.SacredLife.com
United States of America

❧ ❧ Sacred Living, Sacred Dying

A Guide to Embracing Life and Death

Sacred Living, Sacred Dying: A Guide to Embracing Life and Death may be purchased or ordered through booksellers or by contacting Sharon Lund at www.sharonlund.com, or www.sacredlife.com.

ISBN: 0-9822331-1-6
ISBN: 978-0-9822331-1-5
Library of Congress Control Number: 2009903771

The information, ideas, and suggestions in this book are not intended as a substitute for professional advice. Before following any suggestions contained in this book, consult your physician or mental health professional. Neither the author nor the publisher shall be liable or responsible for any loss or damage allegedly arising as a consequence of your use or application of any information or suggestions in this book.

Cover and text design: Miko Radcliffe
Cover photo: Jeaneen Lund

Sacred Life Publishers™
www.SacredLife.com
Printed in the United States of America

For my beautiful, precious daughter

Jeaneen

whose eternal love

brought me back to life.

Sharon Lund

❧   ❧

Sacred Living, Sacred Dying

A Guide to Embracing Life and Death

Contents

❧   ❧

Chapter 1
Legacy of Love

Chapter 2
Saying Goodbye

భ   ఆ

Chapter 3
Decisions You Must Make

☙   ❧

Chapter 4
Important Information Needed Upon Your Death

ᘐ   ᘏ

Chapter 5
Sharon's Near-Death Experience (NDE)

ᘐ   ᘏ

Appendix

Foreword by
Stephen and Ondrea Levine

For some years, we have suggested the experiment in consciousness described in *A Year To Live: How to Live This Year As If It Were Your Last.* Thousands of people have committed themselves to this life-enhancing, business-finishing preparation for death, which so clarifies the preciousness and further potentials for life. Several dozen groups formed together to share this process of coming more fully alive. And some came to this experiment in consciousness because it was indeed their final months or days. I wish I had Sharon Lund's *Sacred Living, Sacred Dying: A Guide to Embracing Life and Death* to round out our practice. With her profound attention to detail, she deals with the practical side of preparing for death as a means of lightening the burden of worry and concern about how one might die with their business finished, with no loose ends, and describing to loved ones, caretakers, physicians, and lawyers how one wishes to be treated in the dying process and afterward. That is why Sharon has chosen in her teachings, books, and groups, to offer the potential power of combining the processes of *A Year to Live* with *Sacred Living, Sacred Dying.*

Sharon knows from deep personal, yet universal, experience of nearing death many times, the power of being prepared. She has confronted AIDS since 1983. She is a very living example that such preparation, of relating so wholeheartedly to death, does not harm but actually increases the life flow that wholeheartedly appreciates life unto the final celebration. Having on at least one occasion a profound near-death experience, the sort that awakens us from our "near-life experience" that draws us back to the center of our lives from which most have long since strayed, she speaks from a rare wisdom and perspective. But we don't have to have some remarkable altered state of consciousness to rediscover our lives. Ironically, the contemplation and even preparation for death leads us back to our center, our heart, our deathless suchness.

From Plato to the Dalai Lama there has been echoed the teaching, "Practice dying!" and part of that process is a devotion to the completion of the practical preparations as an act of compassion so as to lighten the burden of those grieving bedside, an accumulation of vital information which for many creates a contemplation of priorities which in itself focuses the mind and furthers the interests of the heart, a crucial ritual to settle the roller-coaster mind, and find some inkling of peace when even a distant, much less an impending, end of life is contemplated. A life history that tends to clear the way for whatever comes next, a kind of catching up with yourself, and even planning into the future, of body honoring, of wishes for the preparation of the body and burial and graveside rituals of connection and heartful parting, without actually getting ahead of ourselves.

If someone approached us kindly, extending their hands in which was cupped our vital life force, we would be most grateful for their gentle handling and the offering up to us of an opportunity to review, and even somewhat direct, the path of that undying luminescence of the stream of life that passes as consciousness through us and eventually flows outward and beyond into unseen realms that only love can breach. Indeed, we might even bow in gratitude to such a messenger, such an angel of mercy. This is just what Sharon Lund extends to us all, an opportunity to live well, to die into the collective heart of loved ones, and leave a sweet aftertaste in appreciative memories of our concern for their well being. Little left incomplete to confuse the parting, with our life whole and ready for the next evolutionary step, whether it is holding your children and lovers of a sweet Saturday evening, or our last breath on Friday night dying into peace.

Stephen and Ondrea Levine
Authors of *Unattended Sorrow;*
A Year to Live: *How to Live This Year as if It Were Your Last,* and *Who Dies?: An Investigation of Conscious Living and Conscious Dying*

❧   ☙

Introduction

Understanding the importance and dignity of the process of dying is a product of my life experience and spiritual journey. I have danced with life and death since early childhood. My early history of abuse, the unexpected losses of family members, my community involvement, as well as my own adult struggle with illness, gradually brought me to write this book about the sacredness of living and dying. With experience and knowledge in a variety of traditions and rituals related to death and dying, I have learned to focus my vision through the lens of each individual's life so I might best support his or her beliefs and traditions. This perspective allows me to guide them to prepare their legacy, their celebration of life, and their transition in a loving and compassionate way.

I was born Sharon Marie Clark in Seattle, Washington, in late November, 1949. I was gifted with my parents, Tom and Jean Clark, who were loving, kind, generous, supportive and encouraging.

I am the second born of four children. Tommy, the oldest, was my hero and friend. My younger brother Raymond was often sick, which precluded us from being close. My sister Joyce is nine years younger than me, and she became my living doll – I loved to take care of her when she was little. Now that we're both adults we cherish our friendship and talk to each other daily.

My parents taught my siblings and me to help people less fortunate than us and to volunteer our time, a theme that threads through my life. Another of the significant lessons my parents taught us was the importance of prayer. As far back as I can remember, I always wanted to sit up front when our family went to church. I thought the closer I was to the priest, the closer I was to God.

From the time I was three until I was twelve years old, my connection to spirit through prayer was strengthened as I endured rape by my grandfather. I prayed every day and night for relief from my grandfather's malicious behavior – silently praying he would die so he couldn't hurt me any more. Being raped took away my innocence and ripped me apart mentally, emotionally, and physically, but I was able to endure by praying. My prayers were answered with the introduction of a Spirit Guide, my Guardian Angel. She told me God sent her, and her loving presence helped me. Every time my grandfather raped me, she lifted me out of my body and took me to fun places. She taught me how we are all connected and how to communicate with the plant, mineral, animal, and spirit kingdoms.

I also found deep comfort with a toy doll I had during my earliest childhood years. This baby doll, whom I named Susie, was the only "person" I could talk to about what was happening to me. My grandfather's harsh, cruel words echoed loudly through my mind, "If you tell anyone I will kill your Mommy." Then when I was twelve years old and my grandfather died suddenly, I felt responsible for his death and this guilt lingered.

Because of my connection to spirit and my desire to deal with my internal turmoil, I chose to go to an all-girls Catholic boarding school during my high school years. At one point I considered becoming a Good Shepherd Nun to devote myself to working with troubled teenage girls; however, what I was really searching for was a deeper connection with Infinite Spirit/God. This connection would come, in time, but not in the way I expected.

In 1969, at the age of nineteen, I married my first husband, Tom. He was in the Army and stationed in Japan. While living as an Army wife in Japan, I worked for the American Red Cross Headquarters at Camp Zama where I scheduled transportation to bring the wounded servicemen and women from Vietnam to our local military hospital. I also made the necessary arrangements so those who chose to have their R&R in Japan could meet their loved ones. Once a week I volunteered in the military hospital doing all I could to comfort, assist, and befriend the wounded servicemen and women.

At the age of twenty-one, I was back living in Seattle and divorced. That same year during Memorial Day weekend, Tommy, my older brother and hero, was killed instantly in a motorcycle accident at the age of twenty-three. To this day, I still miss his physical presence, but I feel his spirit around me.

If the death of one brother was not enough, when I was twenty-six my younger brother Raymond died of an overdose of heroin. He, like Tommy, was twenty-three years old when he died.

In 1983, I married my second husband, Bill. After six months of mental and emotional abuse culminating in anorexia, I left him. I was so ill from anorexia I could not take care of my beloved daughter from my first marriage, Jeaneen, who was then eight years old. I sent her to live with my parents in Maui where she would also spend time with her father and his parents.

After Jeaneen was in a safe place with loved ones and I knew she was being taken care of, I starved myself, stayed in isolation, and sat in the house with the curtains drawn. My mind had been overwhelmed by the abuse from my grandfather and Bill. I decided the only way to stop my suffering was to end my life.

My first attempt at suicide was unsuccessful; I threw up the full bottle of pills I had swallowed. A few days later, I leaned against the bathroom tub and placed a sharp, shiny razor on my left wrist. I said my final prayers, asked to be forgiven for what I was about to do, and asked God to let me know if there was anything I needed to know before I killed myself. Instantly the bathroom filled up with brilliant, warm, soothing, loving light. Telepathically, I heard, *"My child, this is not your time to die. Get yourself into the hospital and when you return you will become a healer, teach around the world, and write books."* None of this made sense to me, but I knew without a doubt this was a message from Infinite Spirit and I had received my life purpose. I immediately allowed my doctor to admit me into an eating-disorder ward. He was relieved to get my call, as he had attempted to convince me for months to go into the hospital.

During my three-month hospital stay, one of our daily assignments was to journal in the mornings and evenings. Within days of my admission I started to write. Information channeled to me from the spirit realm poured out. I was introduced to one of my main Spirit Guides, who is still with me today. He taught me the basics of the spiritual world and the nature of Spirit Guides, along with Native American Traditions. Shortly after this meeting, one night at the foot of my hospital bed, a different Spirit Being appeared before me. By the name and appearance of this Spirit Being, I knew he was Japanese. He told me he came to teach me Eastern philosophy and healing techniques. In Spring 2000, this Spirit Being told me he needed to leave because I had learned all that he came to teach me. (My Spirit Guides have not taken the place of Infinite Spirit. I see them as working with God.)

After my three months of treatment in the hospital, I was eager to bring Jeaneen home and start enjoying my life with her again. My heart was filled with joy. Our love, embraces, talks, and time together became even more meaningful and sacred as I shared with her the teachings I learned.

In Los Angeles during the first part of 1985, I met my mentor, Linda Dutton-Steindler, who taught me visualization, meditation, affirmations, various healing modalities, the importance of positive attitude and thoughts, emotional clearing, and how to listen to my body. She also introduced me to my inner child and other ways to enhance my well-being, which made a profound difference in my life and inner wisdom. My heart, mind, soul, and spirit embraced all the information I was given. Everything Linda taught me was new, yet it resonated deep within me.

The year 1986 was a significant one for me. I started volunteering in the cancer and AIDS communities in Los Angeles teaching the various body-mind-spirit healing techniques I had learned to people faced with life challenging illnesses. I also did healing energy work on men who were infected with AIDS.

That same year I became an ordained New Thought Minister. Through my studies, I learned about various religions around the world, but more importantly, I embraced spirituality finding a new way to accept, relate, and communicate to people and the world. I felt a deeper connection to all, becoming a more spiritual being, realizing God is within me. Through my spirituality, I experience inner peace, higher wisdom, and clarity about things I had so often questioned before, which I still honor today.

Christmas 1986 my parents came to spend the holiday with Jeaneen and me. They didn't like my working on men infected with AIDS, especially if they had KS (Kaposi's Sarcoma), because they were afraid Jeaneen and I would become infected. My plan was to educate my parents about the myths and realities of HIV/AIDS. Before I could embark on my plan, however, they showed me Dan Rather's T.V. special report, *"AIDS Hits Home,"* which they had taped a few months earlier. Minutes into the tape, to my horror and my parents' surprise, I saw my ex-husband Bill announcing to the television audience he was bi-sexual and infected with AIDS. My parents had not recognized Bill when they first saw the show. Not only had they met him just once in 1983, but CBS had attempted to protect Bill's privacy by semi-obscuring his face on the TV special.

I confronted Bill and he denied he had been on the AIDS special. In meditation I heard it was Bill, and I needed to be tested. My test came back positive for being infected. Already active in the AIDS community made it easier for me to accept this news, yet I went into denial. I thought nothing would ever happen to me. I had never heard of a woman infected with HIV/AIDS before, let alone met one.

Shortly after my diagnosis, I went to an AIDS specialist and he told me I had to go on a new drug, AZT, which had just come out on the market, or I would die within six months. The next day in my morning meditation I asked if it was for my highest good to take the drug and I heard, *"No. Do not take AZT."*

I figured since I was not going to take the AZT, I would die within 6 months and I needed to get all my affairs in order. I asked my parents, once again, if they would bring up Jeaneen, then eleven, when I died. A few weeks later, I heard in meditation, *"Why have you made your doctor God? Why have you bought into this doctor's death sentence? He does not know how or when you are going to die."*

That was an immediate wake-up call. I fired my doctor and found a holistic doctor, a woman who established a partnership with me and respected my decisions. She convinced me to go public with my story about being infected so I could help other people understand the myths and realities of HIV/AIDS. When I broke my silence and spoke my truth, I became stronger.

This led to years of teaching around the world, which fulfilled part of my life purpose given to me during my suicide attempt. I gave presentations throughout the United States, then in Canada, Russia, Europe, and Japan. I spoke about HIV/AIDS, alternative therapies, eating disorders, spirituality, and sacred living sacred dying. My life experiences were the catalyst for appearances on *The Oprah Winfrey Show, 48 Hours, Eye on America, CNN*, and other national television shows. Part of my life story was featured in the November 2007 issue of "O" The Oprah Magazine.

In 1989, Bill called me a few days before he died from AIDS complications and finally admitted he was infected prior to marrying me and had led a secret bi-sexual life. He told me I needed to be tested. (Of course, I already had been tested three years earlier when I saw him on the AIDS special.)

I did not allow people to treat me as an innocent victim because of how I became infected. My motto became, "It doesn't matter how any man, woman, or child becomes infected, we all deserve the same compassion, love, and understanding."

Being infected with the virus empowered me. It taught me the importance of being responsible for my life and well-being. I no longer take life for granted. I take better care of myself, and I am living my life purpose. I have always been spiritual, but I believe my spirituality expanded to greater depths.

In 1990, I became HIV-symptomatic. I experienced extreme fatigue, weight loss, fevers, drenching night sweats, memory problems, diarrhea, and other problems. At one point, Jeaneen became the mother and I became the child. That forced me to come out of denial – thinking I would never get sick. This led me to experience the five stages of DABDA that the late Elisabeth Kübler-Ross spoke about (denial, anger, bargain, depression, and then acceptance). Once I regained my strength, Jeaneen became a teen peer AIDS educator, and from time to time we would give presentations together.

As I continued to work in the AIDS and cancer communities, I was filled with profound gratitude, respect, appreciation, compassion, understanding, and love for all that life holds as well as the sacredness and beauty of death. However, after years of being active in the AIDS community, from 1986 to 1993, and witnessing so many dear friends die from AIDS complications, I was stricken by survivor's guilt. It took a lot of inner work and therapy to overcome it. Eventually, I realized my life still had a purpose and I needed to stay healthy and strong to achieve it. I had to let go of my survivor's guilt and live so the men, women, and children who had died from AIDS complications would have their memories live on through my work.

By the spring of 1993, I was burned out from volunteering locally, nationally, and internationally, and I heard in my meditation that I needed to slow down or I would become sick again. I decided to move out of Los Angeles. I moved first to Westlake Village, an hour north of Los Angeles, and a year later I was told to move to the red rocks for healing. Once again, I trusted what I heard in meditation, and I was Divinely guided to my new home surrounded by the magnificent red rocks of Kayenta, ten minutes outside of St. George, Utah. Within a short amount of time, I became active on the Southern Utah AIDS Task Force, helped set up their AIDS walk, and presented a few HIV/AIDS educational presentations.

To my horror, 1996 turned into a nightmare. I became infected with PCP (Pneumocystis carinii Pneumonia) and MAI/MAC (Mycobacterium Avium Intracellular infection), which are two of the deadliest viruses for people infected with AIDS. For over a year, I was in the hospital more than I was out. My sister, Joyce, left her home in Arizona and came to live with me. She took care of me whenever I was not in the hospital.

In March 1997, after a year and a half of being sick due to AIDS complications, I had my near-death experience, which I share in detail in Chapter 5.

Four days into 1999, once again death took away another member of my family. My loving Mom, after years of having difficulty with each breath she took, died of emphysema.

As you can tell by now, I have danced with life and death throughout my life, and each challenge seeded the gifts and wisdom I share with you in this book. By facing all of my challenges and releasing them, they have become sacred because they have healed me, brought me to self-discovery and wholeness, and to living my life purpose.

Throughout the decades, I have served men and women worldwide who have died from AIDS complications, cancer, other life-challenging illnesses, unexpected events, or old age. I am honored to have participated in their final celebrations of life and to have been present at their bedsides as they made their transitions. Some of these people were not prepared for death, which was devastating for them and their loved ones. Having grown to appreciate the sacredness of life and death, my passion is to assist other men and women to leave their legacy and plan a unique memorial. By honoring the story of our life's journey and sharing our wisdom, we will discover ways for our memories to live on in the hearts and minds of friends and loved ones.

I ask you to open your heart and mind and journey with me to a place perhaps you have never been before, and you, too, will have an opportunity to embrace life and death in a very sacred way.

Love and Blessings to You,

Sharon Lund

Suggestions

It's only when we truly know and understand that we have a limited time on earth – and that we have no way of knowing when our time is up, we will then begin to live each day to the fullest, as if it was the only one we had.

~ Elisabeth Kübler-Ross[1]

Sacred Living, Sacred Dying: A Guide to Embracing Life and Death is not necessarily a book to be read from cover to cover. You may do a quick overview and find you want to come back to some sections and disregard others. You have the freedom to explore different ideas to create your life story and your memorial or celebration of life.[2]

As you read through the chapters that resonate with you, there might be items or questions you want to return to. Later you may want to make notes to refresh your memory when you start to create your *Sacred Planner: Your Legacy of Love and Final Wishes.* Or, you may purchase your personal workbook through my website at www.sharonlund.com.

You may feel overwhelmed by answering some of the questions. However, you can pick and choose what questions you want to

---

[1] For information about Elisabeth Kübler-Ross please go to www.elisabethkublerross.com or www.ekrfoundation.org.

[2] When you read "memorial" or "celebration of life," you can replace it with the word funeral.

answer and how you want to answer them for your friends and loved ones.

The most important aspect of this sacred gift, your *Sacred Planner*, is that you take time to reflect on your memories, traditions, wisdom, accomplishments, and values, since they are aspects of your legacy to be shared beyond your days.

Before you venture into your *Sacred Planner,* find a quiet, comfortable environment (indoors or outdoors), where you will feel safe, and not rushed. You may want to light a candle and have your favorite music playing in the background.

The first step in preparing your *Sacred Planner*, entitled *Legacy of Love*, will be collecting personal and fun information, about which you will probably enjoy reminiscing. This section will lead you through practical, spiritual, and emotional questions designed to assist you to create the first portion of your *Sacred Planner* – the story of your life's journey and experiences. Some questions may startle you, and as a result, you may discover you want to start reprioritizing things, people, and events in your life. When your *Legacy of Love* is complete, instead of putting this section of your *Sacred Planner* away until your memorial or celebration of life, you may want to give a copy of the story of your life's journey to a family member, friend, or loved one.

Before you move on to the second part of the *Sacred Planner*, which outlines various ways to create a unique celebration, take a moment to look outside the box of society, which frames a memorial after death. It might feel liberating to have your celebration of life happen while you are alive so you can physically be part of this sacred day – a day to honor your precious life! You could sit back and witness all you created and embrace the thoughts and memories your friends and loved ones have for you and you for them. You don't have to wait for your memorial or celebration of life until after you die. The choice is yours.

Throughout the chapters *Saying Goodbye* and *Decisions You Must Make*, you will be looking at legalities and choices you must make before your transition. As you go through these sections, you may experience emotions ranging from sadness to happiness to joy to frustration. Whatever you feel is real, so don't minimize your feelings. Allow them to come forth. If you need support, reach out to a loved one, friend, clergy member, or therapist.

Know that the amount of time you spend creating the second part of your *Sacred Planner* will spare your friends and loved ones from having to make critical and often difficult decisions at the emotional time of your death. Carefully go through each category and, if you wish, discuss your thoughts and feelings regarding your wishes with those closest to you. Then choose the things that represent who you are, and be as detailed as you want to be.

You can write[3], type, video, or audio tape your *Legacy of Love* and final wishes. Some people choose to have a combination of a printed copy and audio or video, so their voice can be heard and their presence can be seen long after they have passed away. If your *Sacred Planner* is in print, I recommend you have it notarized and kept with the rest of your important documents. The only place you don't want to keep it is in your safe deposit box which is usually sealed immediately upon death and cannot be opened until

---

[3] Note that throughout *Sacred Living, Sacred Dying* the words "write or type" may be used, but that reference also extends to putting your *Sacred Planner* on audio or videotape. Sometimes we may be unable to write our own *Sacred Planner* and may require assistance. If you have a special friend or loved one – someone you trust, respect, and feel comfortable – then ask that person to assist you with your *Sacred Planner*. They can ask you the questions throughout the book; then write, type, video or audio tape your answers to the questions. Having them help with your *Sacred Planner* might be one of the most meaningful times the two of you spend together.

released by the court. So share the existence of your *Sacred Planner* with the loved ones responsible for your final arrangements, and tell them where it is located.

For a printed copy, some people choose to use a flexible binder, bound with sheet protectors built in and a clear front view. If you choose a binder, make your cover as simple or elaborate as you desire. You can decorate the front with a nice design, insert a picture or a photo that captures the essence of you, or simply write words such as: *My Life Story, My Sacred Journey, My Gift of Life, My Celebration of Life, Sacred Passages,* or anything you like. Your *Sacred Planner* is a representation of you and your life, so allow your personality to come forth.

As you gather information, such as brochures, documents, and poems pertaining to your wishes about your memorial or celebration of life, you may want to place them in the back of your *Sacred Planner* so they will be available for your loved ones when they are needed.

You may decide to update your *Sacred Planner* from time to time. As new people enter your life and your circumstances change, you will want your life story and your memorial or celebration of life to reflect your current relationships and situations. In addition, as children become older, different memories may be more appropriate than when you first made your *Sacred Planner*.

You can start your *Sacred Planner* with an introduction (an example is on the next page) and then lead into your vital information. From there, you will move into creating the story of your life and make all of your wishes and desires known. Once you begin, you will discover you can accomplish a lot in a couple of hours.

Example of an introduction:

℘   ℘

The Sacred Life and Celebration

of

(Your Name)

Sample

To My Loved Ones...

My journey through life has been filled with wonderful people, memories, and experiences. As you read the pages of my *Sacred Planner*, you will be embracing the very essence of my life and my love for you. Also included throughout these pages is my personal information and details concerning the final celebration of my life. I give this as a sacred gift to you because it represents me.

It is my hope as you review this *Sacred Planner* that it will serve as a valuable reference and will alleviate some of the burden and any confusion regarding my final farewell. Please know this was carefully, thoughtfully, and sincerely prepared with you in mind. I leave it in your care, along with my loving thoughts.

Know Dear Ones you are deeply loved.

_____

(Your complete legal signature)

_____

Date

Chapter 1

Legacy of Love

❧ ❧

About You

In your *Sacred Planner,* share things that are special to you so your family, friends, and loved ones may also enjoy them! Listed below are different categories of questions you may want to write about. Feel free to create your own dialogue and questions about special things, people, events, and circumstances in your life.

❖ Begin your *Legacy of Love* by writing your personal introduction, and then on the next page start *About You,* including your legal name. In addition, if you have any fun or interesting nicknames, include them. Mention how your nicknames came about.

❖ How young are you? Tell your friends and loved ones your birth date and where you were born. If you heard any stories about your birth, include them.

❖ As you reflect on your childhood, write about your earliest memories. Describe your first childhood friendships. What did you enjoy doing as a child? What was your favorite toy(s)? Did you have a special name for it? Who gave it to you? Who was your hero? Where was your favorite place to visit and why? What was your favorite radio or TV show and game? Did you have any pets? If so, describe their personalities and behaviors. What did you name them?

❖ What comes to mind when you think about your adolescent years? What did you enjoy doing as an adolescent? When you were young, what did you want to be when you grew up? At what age where you attracted to the opposite sex? Who was your first love interest? What did you like about him or her? What did you enjoy doing together?

❖ As you reminisce about your school days, what stands out in your mind? What was school like for you? What activities, sports, and clubs were you involved in? What was your favorite subject and why? What was your least favorite subject and why? What was your favorite grade? What made it your favorite grade in school? Which teacher most aided your journey in school and how? Who was your closest friend(s) in school? What did you enjoy doing together? What was your favorite music group(s)?

❖ What age were you when you obtained your first car, truck, or motorcycle? What was the make, year, model, and color of it? How much did your first car, truck, or motorcycle cost? Where did you enjoy going?

❖ Who was your first date? What was your first date like? Where did you go? What did you do? What did you like about this person? Did you go out with this person again, if so for how long?

❖ Looking back at your home environment, what feelings did you experience there? What lasting impressions did your home environment leave in your mind? What did you enjoy doing in and around your home? If there were special things about your home, write about them.

❖ When you lived at home, what skills did you learn that enhanced your adult life, such as cooking, gardening, sewing, caring for a child, fixing or building items?

Now expand your memories to include your journey throughout life and share heartfelt memories:

4

❖ Write about your closest friend(s). This might be someone you have known most of your life, or it might be a new-found friend. What kind of personality does he or she have and what makes them your closest friend? Does he or she live nearby or do you have a long distance friendship? What kinds of things do you enjoy doing together? Tell how the two of you bring out the best in each other.

❖ To expand your circle of friends, mention three people who helped you through difficult times and in what way they assisted you.

❖ To whom do you owe appreciation? Who makes you feel appreciated and special? How do they show it?

❖ In your lifetime, who has been your strongest inspiration and why? It might be a family member, a teacher, or someone famous like Martin Luther King Jr., Mother Teresa, or Gandhi.

❖ Let people know what you are passionate about and what gives your life meaning. What do you find fascinating? For what are you most grateful? What is one of the happiest days of your life or your proudest moment? What are some of your most memorable experiences and adventures?

❖ Tell your friends and loved ones about organizations or clubs to which you belong(ed). What did you like most about them and how did you contribute?

❖ It is important to honor people's lives by sharing achievements. Write about your special achievements, accomplishments, or awards. It doesn't matter if you didn't climb Mt. Everest or win the Nobel Peace Prize; a good life is a great achievement.

❖ Write about the personality traits you think most people recognize in you. Perhaps it's your sense of humor, your work ethic, your stubbornness, or something else. Show how your different personality traits come out in your life.

❖ People respond to experiences differently. What comes to mind when you answer these questions: What makes you happy? What makes you sad? What frustrates you? What do you fear most in life? What does crying mean to you? Is it okay for you to cry? How do you feel or respond when someone else cries?

❖ People are faced with challenges during their lifetimes. What has been your greatest challenge(s)? Who or what has been your support during your trying times? What have been your major turning points in your life? What is your biggest regret in life? What major lessons have you learned from overcoming your challenges?

❖ When the world seems dark and gloomy, or you are down and out, what one thing always lifts your spirits and makes you happy? It might be your favorite music, the voice of a loved one, walking in nature, playing ball, or taking a long hot bath.

❖ Share your fondest memory and funniest moment.

❖ What was an embarrassing moment you could laugh about later?

❖ Something you may not know about me is . . . (fill in the blank).

❖ It might surprise you to know . . . (fill in the blank).

❧   ❧

Some of Your Favorite Things

Write down some of your favorite things.

❖ What hobbies do/did you enjoy? What is your favorite food?

❖ What color makes you happy? In your wardrobe, what color brings out the best in you?

❖ What sound is pleasing to your ears? What sound annoys you?

❖ What is your favorite word? What does this word mean to you?

❖ What is your favorite time of day and why? What do you enjoy doing or not doing during that time of day?

❖ Write about your favorite book and movie and why they are your favorites.

❖ Where is your favorite place to go? What makes this place special? What do you enjoy doing there?

❖ Share your favorite type of music. If you have any special artists (singers or groups) list who they are. What songs touch your heart and why?

❖ There are countless fabulous, inspirational, and funny sayings. If there are any poignant ones you like, share them in your *Sacred Planner*.

❖ Do you have a favorite art piece, jewelry, or something you created that is special to you? What is it and why is it special?

❖ In your lifetime have you had a favorite pet? If so, what is his/her name and what is special about this pet?

❧   ☙

Past or Present Profession

Throughout your life you may have held various kinds of jobs, or perhaps you focused on necessary steps that led you to your major career.

❖ Let your memory go back in time and tell your friends and loved ones about your first real job. How old were you? How did the job come about? How did you get to and from work? What did you do at your job? How much money did you make per hour, week, or month? What did you learn from your first job that helped you in any of your other professions?

❖ Write about your main occupation. Where you work(ed), the location, your title, what you do or did there, and how many years you worked at this job. Were there any necessary steps you had to take in order to obtain your job? What do or did you enjoy most about your job or career? What is your proudest career accomplishment?

❖ What profession, other than your own, would you have liked to attempt? What profession would be least appealing to you?

❖ Were you in the military? If so, what branch of service? What dates did you serve your country? If you were not drafted, why did you join the military? Why did you choose your branch of service? Whether you served in peace time or in war, share some of your experiences while serving your country. Did you receive any medals? If so, for what? You may want to write down the names of your medals and the reasons for receiving them. Perhaps you would like to have your well-deserved medals displayed at your memorial or celebration of life. If so, state where they are located.

❖ If you're not retired, what are you looking forward to doing in your Golden Years?

❖ If you're retired, what do you enjoy doing now that you weren't able to do when you were working? What do you still want to do that you haven't yet done?

Your Spouse, Partner, Lover

Take your time to write about the special person you hold dearest to your heart. It doesn't matter if he or she is alive or deceased; they still hold a sacred or loving memory.

❖ Do/did you have a significant other?

❖ What is/was his or her name?

❖ How long have/had you been together?

❖ Where and how did you meet?

❖ What personality traits drew you to this person?

❖ What do/did you find interesting about him or her?

❖ What is/was special in your heart about this person?

❖ At what point did you know he or she was the person who captured your heart?

❖ How do/did you enhance each others' lives?

❖ What things do/did you enjoy doing together?

❖ What is the greatest thing he or she has done for you?

❖ What one thing would you like to see the two of you accomplish or what did you accomplish together?

❖ How do you feel loved? What speaks to your heart? What is your language of love?

⤻   ⤸

Generations of Family and Love

The word "family" can mean different things to different people. When you think of family who comes to mind?

❖   Write some interesting things about your family members, living and deceased. You may want to list their full names and your relationship to them.

❖   What are/were their personality traits?

❖   What role and impact do/did they have or had in your life?

❖   Where do/did they live? Do/did you visit each other? If so, what is/was it like spending time together?

❖   When you were growing up were you closer to one of your siblings than another? If so, with whom, and what made you closer?

❖   How might you be more present in your current relationships?

As you recall special holidays such as New Year's, Easter, Mother's Day, Cinco de Mayo, Father's Day, the 4th of July, Halloween, Thanksgiving, Hanukkah, Bodhi Day, Christmas, the various Solstices, or other special days, are there traditions your family carried out when you were growing up which you continue to honor? Or are there special rituals you started after you left home?

❖ For New Year's – do/did you enjoy parties and staying up until the clock ticks midnight? Or do/did you enjoy bringing the New Year in with ritual and stillness or silence?

❖ On the 4th of July – do/did you have a family gathering where you have/had a barbeque or picnic? Is/was it a tradition to watch the fireworks?

❖ Thanksgiving – do/did you help feed the homeless and then have a traditional dinner with loved ones?

❖ Christmas – do/did you stroll around the neighborhood with friends singing carols or play in the snow? Do/did you sponsor a family during the holidays?

Write about your holidays (past and present) and include any rituals you enjoyed. What is it like to be together with your family or be apart from them during the holidays?

If you have a child, children, grandchildren, or niece(s) and nephew(s), what special moments come to mind when you think about them concerning the holidays?

You may choose to write about your extended family, the community you belong to, or your circle of friends. What important aspect do they play in your life? List a couple of traits that best characterize them. Give an example of times when you witnessed these qualities.

As you look at your relationships with friends and loved ones, what relationships have you left incomplete? What would it take for you to feel a sense of completion and peace?

Now that you have reflected on your generations of family, are there any communications you have left unsaid with your friends or loved ones? If so, it is never too late to communicate your feelings, even if the person has died. You can visualize the person and have the conversation you need with them. Or perhaps you would like to write a letter to them and then burn it, which symbolizes releasing those feelings. Do whatever it takes to feel at peace.

Your pets are family members too, so share your pet(s) name(s) and write about how your pet(s) came into your life and the difference they made. When you close your eyes and think about your pet(s) what makes you smile? What do/did you always count on your pet(s) to do or not do?

❧   ❧

Your Feelings about Religion, Spirituality, and Death

Everyone has different feelings about death, religion, and spirituality, and these topics are seldom discussed. Take the time to answer the following questions.

❖ Do you believe in a Higher Power? If so, what do you call your Higher Power?

❖ Do you follow a certain religion, spirituality, or philosophy? If so, what is it?

❖ If you belong to a congregation, write the name, address, and phone number of your congregation. Who is the presiding person such as priest, minister, rabbi, guru? Do you have a special connection to this person? If so, what is it and why? What experiences do you have with the members of the congregation and how do you relate to them?

❖ Do you believe there is a difference between religion and spirituality? If so, explain.

❖ What does faith mean to you?

❖ Do you connect in some way with a larger perspective of life?

No one knows when their last breath of life will occur, so take a slow deep breath and search your heart as you answer the following questions.

16

❖ Are you afraid of death or the dying process? If so, why? If not, why?

❖ Do you believe in life after death or reincarnation?

❖ What would be your reaction or response to receiving a one-year-to-live prognosis?

❖ Are you at peace with your life? If not, what will it take to be at peace?

❖ Why do you think you are living, and is this life anything like you thought it would be?

❖ What would you consider an ideal way to die?

❖ What do you anticipate death to be like?

❖ When you die, what would you want God or your Higher Power to telepathically say to you?

If...

Let your imagination soar. The only limitation is the one you place on it. If money, fitness, time, education, and age were not issues, take a moment to allow your mind to wonder and think about the following questions.

- ❖ If neither money nor time were an issue, what would you want to do and why?

- ❖ If you could visit anywhere in the world, where would you travel and why?

- ❖ If you could sit down and visit three people (alive or deceased), who would you choose to enjoy spending your time with and why?

- ❖ If you could start all over at a new career, what would it be and why?

- ❖ If money were no object, what one thing would you purchase that would bring you joy and why?

- ❖ If volunteering your time brings about a deep sense of gratitude and joy, where or for whom would you be volunteering and why?

- ❖ If you could help humanity in the greatest way, what way would it be?

❖ If you could change one thing in your life, what would it be and why?

❖ If you could change one thing in the world, what would it be and why?

❖ If you could make one wish, what would it be and why?

❖ If you could have more control over one thing in your life, what would it be and why?

❖ If there were people you hurt in some way, whom you wanted forgiveness from, who are they? What would you say?

❖ If there were people who hurt you in some way and you needed or wanted to forgive them, who are they? What would you say or do?

❖ If you could show the same gratitude for unpleasant experiences as you do for pleasant experiences, what would that look like?

Now realize no one knows the moment of their last breath, so answer the following questions thoughtfully.

❖ If you approached illness as an experiment in staying present, how might that change your attitude?

❖ If you knew you only had a year to live, would you live your life differently? If so, how?

❖ If you knew you only had 90 days to live, what would you do during those final three precious months of your life?

❖ If you were to be remembered for only one thing what would you like that to be and why?

❧   ☙

Your Wisdom and Gifts

Each person is unique in their own way, and has special wisdom and gifts. Allow yourself to go within your heart to share your special wisdom and gifts with your friends and loved ones.

❖   What wisdom have you learned that you would like to pass on?

❖   What have you accomplished in this lifetime that could benefit future generations?

❖   What gift do you wish to give to your succeeding generations?

❖   How do you wish you could be better and at what?

❖   What is your greatest blessing in life?

❖   What is your source of joy?

❖   What do you think are the three greatest inventions in the world and why?

❖   What is one of the greatest gifts you have ever given someone?

❖   What is one of the greatest gifts you have ever received?

❖   Who or what has been your greatest influence (good and bad) in your life?

❖ What does freedom mean to you?

❖ What are three important ingredients for a great relationship? Are these present in your life?

❖ What is your favorite thing a person could do for you?

❖ What do you enjoy doing for others?

❖ What is your life purpose? Why? Are you living it? If not, why not?

* * *

The lists could go on and on as you tell the story of your life. This outline gives you some ideas about the precious things you may choose to write about in your *Legacy of Love.*

You might want to make your *Legacy of Love* available to the person who will give your eulogy.

Once your *Legacy of Love* is created, you have embraced the sacredness of your life's journey. Now you have an opportunity to embrace death as you move into the next section of your *Sacred Planner, Saying Goodbye,* where you will begin to create a unique memorial or celebration, honoring the story of your life.

Chapter 2

Saying Goodbye

Set the Tone?

This is the final celebration of your life. Think about it for a moment. If you could suggest it, what kind of feeling or tone would you set for your memorial? Some people prefer a somber tone, paying their final respects through mourning; others prefer a joyous celebration of their life—their last big party.

Whatever choices you make, sadness and tears are inevitable. Give your friends and loved ones the tools they need to honor your life in a positive way. Describe what tone you would like to have at your memorial or celebration of life. Remember the cumulative experience of your life means much more than the day of your death.

Traditionally people wear black to funerals, but perhaps you would rather state in your *Sacred Planner* that the people attending your memorial wear something bright and cheerful, or maybe even your favorite color.

If you have a special time of day such as the tranquil mornings, high noon, or the beautiful sunset, you may choose to have your memorial at that time of day, in honor of you.

Maybe you would like to create a theme that represents you and your interests, such as dance, fishing, golf, angels, eagles, nature, crystals, or flowers. Or you may want to consider a western, cultural, or international theme such as Indian, Japanese, Chinese, or Tibetan.

Where Will You Say Goodbye?

Usually when people think of a memorial or reception, they think of a church, cathedral, chapel, synagogue, or mortuary. Think for a moment about the meaningful locations in your life. What places really bring you happiness and represent who you are, or reflect a part of your life?

❖ Perhaps your final farewell would be outdoors. Maybe you enjoy being near water, or out on a boat. Maybe your favorite place is a spacious green park, or in the middle of a beautiful meadow in the countryside. You could have your celebration in the mountains, out in the open desert, near a river, or on the first tee of your favorite golf course.

❖ Or do you like being indoors more? If so, you may prefer to have your memorial or celebration of life at your favorite restaurant, museum, casino, a club, or organization to which you belong.

Read the following paragraph and then close your eyes for a moment.

Think about the one place that brings you the most joy. When you think of that place, notice how your body feels. Perhaps you feel excitement and delight and you catch yourself smiling. The place you are thinking about, right now, might be the perfect location to have your memorial or celebration of life. Consider exploring the option to make your memorial or celebration of life happen at this special place.

The Music of Your Life

Music has the power to set the tone and ambience of an occasion. What atmosphere do you want? Everyone has favorite songs and music. What are yours? Have them played during your visitation, memorial, celebration of life, reception, or your final resting place. Let people listen to the music and songs which hold a special meaning for you. In addition, you might want someone to explain why particular songs are important. You may also want to have a song dedicated to a friend or loved one.

Your selection of songs or music is a very personal choice. The music doesn't have to reflect a traditional visitation or memorial, but if you would like it to do so, the following examples may help:

❖ Perhaps you would like a traditional song like the *Lord's Prayer, Ave Maria,* or *Amazing Grace.*

❖ Some favorite (Christian) hymns are: *The Lord is My Shepherd, Abide With Me, Be Thou My Vision, Dear Lord and Father of Mankind, Come Let Us Join Our Friends Above,* or *Give the Wind Thy Fears.*

❖ If you have served in the military or you enjoy patriotic songs, here is a list of some songs and hymns you may want to think about using: *God Bless America, America the Beautiful, The National Anthem (The Star-Spangled Banner), Battle Hymn of the Republic, A New Wind A-Blowin, Anchors Aweigh, The Caissons Go Rolling Along, The Marines' Hymn,* or *You're A Grand Old Flag.*

❖ If classical music brings joy to your soul, you may want to consider Beethoven's *Adagio from Piano Sonata No. 14 in C*, Chopin's *Sonata No. 2 in B flat "Funeral Sonata"*, Mozart's *Requiem, Pachelbel's Canon in D Major*, or Vivaldi's *Four Seasons*.

❖ Some popular songs that might interested you: Boyz 2 Men, *One Sweet Day,* The Beatles, *The Long and Winding Road,* Phil Collins, *You'll be in My Heart,* Celine Dion, *My Heart Will Go On,* Simon and Garfunkel, *Bridge Over Troubled Water,* Josh Groban, *To Where You Are*, Josh Groban and Charlotte Church, *The Prayer,* Whitney Houston, *I Will Always Love You,* Barry Manilow or Barbra Streisand, *Memory,* Sarah McLachlan, *In the Arms of an Angel,* Led Zeppelin, *Stairway to Heaven.*

❖ Or maybe you enjoy country music and would like a special song sung by a country artist, such as Alabama, *Goodbye,* Johnny Cash, *Cross Over Jordan,* Dixie Chicks, *Godspeed,* Faith Hill, *There You'll Be,* Lee Ann Womack, *I Hope You Dance.*

❖ You may choose to reflect on fond memories and sentimental feelings from a song sung by Perry Como, *Lili Marlene,* Bing Crosby, *Moonlight Becomes You,* Tommy Dorsey or Dinah Shore, *Something to Remember You By,* Frank Sinatra, *I Think of You.*

❖ If you want to travel back to the Big Band era, you may decide to choose music from some of the most famous bands such as: Tommy and Jimmy Dorsey, Glenn Miller, Glen Gray, and Charlie Spivak.

❖ Music from Perry Como, Bing Crosby, Benny Goodman, Spike Jones, Stan Kenton, Frank Sinatra, Andrew Sisters, and Rudy Vallee was also popular.

❖ There are also famous older black musicians and singers to consider, such as Louie Armstrong, Nat King Cole, Duke Ellington, Ella Fitzgerald, Dizzie Gillespie, Billy Holiday, and Charlie Parker.

❖ If you choose the symbolic releasing of your Spirit with doves or butterflies, you might want to choose Celine Dion, *Fly,* Bette Midler, *Wind Beneath My Wings,* or Charley Pride, *Wings of a Dove.*

These are just a few ideas to help you find the right music. Listen to the music and find what lifts your spirit. You may choose to have a selection of songs or music played, or you may decide to skip it. The choice is yours. That's the freedom of your expression when you plan your own memorial or celebration of life.

Also, if you know an individual, group, quartet, or choir you would like to have sing at your memorial, write down their contact information and what you would like them to sing.

Perhaps you know people who play an instrument such as the harp, piano, guitar, bagpipes, fiddle, flute, sax, steel drum, or organ and would like them to perform at your memorial, reception, or final resting place. If so, write down their name(s), phone number, e-mail address, website, and what you would like them to play.

The Poetry of Your Life

There are countless beautiful, inspirational, and uplifting poems and prayers available for your use. If you have favorite ones, you may choose to have someone read them aloud at your memorial or celebration of life. You may also want to have a poem dedicated to a friend or loved one.

If you use the Internet, you can go to Google.com and type in *Poems on Death and Dying.* There you will be able to view a wide selection of poetry. There are hundreds of poems, traditional, general, religious, poems about other people, personal felt poems, and poems about people facing illness. As you navigate through the pages, notice which poems you are drawn to and consider using them during your ceremony.

More importantly, if you have any favorite poems or prayers, share those with your friends and loved ones, because those poems and prayers have touched you in some way. Also let them know why they are your favorites and how they touched you.

စ္စ   ဖ္ဗ

Your Favorite Mementos Displayed

You may choose to have a display of personal mementos that reflect your life story. These items can be displayed at your visitation, memorial, celebration of life, or reception.

Some things you may want to consider displaying are your military service medals, trophies, diplomas, or awards. If you enjoy(ed) sports, you may want to display your sports uniform or equipment such as your golf clubs, snow or water skies, racket, fishing pole, surfboard, Harley Davidson, or favorite dance shoes. You may want to display some pictures you painted, a quilt you made, travel mementos, religious objects, arrangements of your favorite photos throughout your life journey, or even drawings your children or grandchildren made.

You may want to display a favorite object as a life symbol and have someone explain why you loved it and how it reflects your personality. You can have any kind of items you would like displayed, as they represent a part of your life.

❧   ☙

A Dedication in Your Name

There are numerous ways you can arrange to have a dedication in your name. Listed below are some ideas:

❖   Numerous parks will accept memorial gifts in your name. You will have to check with the park of your choice and ask for their prices. You could choose to have the park plant a tree in honor of your life. In addition, there are parks that will allow you to purchase a bench or picnic table in your name. Usually a plaque would be placed on the bench or picnic table, or at the base of the site.

❖   At your local city or county parks department, you can also purchase equipment and have a memorial plaque with your name placed upon it.

❖   Maybe you would like to have a beautiful fountain purchased and placed in a location that has special meaning to you.

❖   An increasingly popular donation is the Automatic External Defibrillator (AED), placed in a community recreation center or senior center. The AED units have proved effective in saving lives of individuals having a heart attack.

❖   You may want to have a stained glass window created in honor of your life and have it installed at your place of worship, or in a loved one's home.

❖   Perhaps you would like to have a foundation named after you, or a scholarship fund set up in honor of your life.

❖ You may want to have a star named after you.

❖ You could have a mass, service, or ritual performed in memory of you.

Below are a few examples of gifts you could choose from through the Internet.

❖ The Gift That Celebrates Life – www.eternitree.com. Eternitree sells easy-to-maintain trees and plants, such as Austrian Pine, Colorado Blue Spruce, Deodara Cedar, Giant Sequoia, Green Mound Juniper, and Bonsai. You may choose to have someone purchase a tree or plant and have it planted in your loved one's yard, or somewhere special to you. Eternitree also sells personal tree markers, flowers, and gift baskets. You can place an order with them through their website or call 609-425-8750.

❖ TreeGivers – www.treegivers.com. This organization will plant a tree in any state or listed country. Each TreeGivers gift tree supplements the natural resources of our Earth and brings life and beauty to the countryside. You can purchase a tree through their website or call 800-862-8733.

❖ Celebration Forest is an American organization which plants trees in a protected forest preserve and dedicates the tree in celebration of your life. Your loved ones will receive a personalized certificate. To order from this company, you can go to their website at www.celebrationforest.com, or call 877-245-7378.

❖ The Comfort Company has a wide variety of garden benches, garden stones, and jewelry, as well as items to dedicate in memory of your pet. You can choose the inscription you would like on these memorial items. Visit their website at www.thecomfortcompany.net to place an order, or you may call them at 630-845-1624.

❖ Exterior Accents has a variety of garden décor such as decorative memorial stones, plaques, or markers you may want placed in a friend's or loved one's garden or walkway. You can choose from a variety of different inscriptions. For more information, visit their website at www.exterior-accents.com/memorialstones.html, where you can see their items and place an order. Or you can call 704-788-2350.

❖ Personal Creations, www.personalcreations.com, provides a variety of unique memorial gifts such as jewelry, memorial stones, candles, ornaments, keepsake boxes, memorial benches, picture frames, poems, and more. Any of these items can be personalized. You can order their merchandise through their website or call 800-326-6626.

These are just a few ideas for having a dedication in your name. You can also search the Internet by going to Google.com and typing *memorial gifts* in the search bar.

❦   ❧

Your Life in Pictures

From the first hospital picture, we capture special moments in photographs. Photo albums may certainly be part of your celebration, but a video or DVD photomontage will present your life in pictures in a unique and special way. The wonderful thing about a video presentation is it celebrates your life in a way your friends and loved ones can view any time. Loved ones can also add more pictures to it before your final celebration viewing. You may also want to arrange to give a copy of your video or DVD to friends and loved ones as a final gift. If this interests you, make it known in your *Sacred Planner*.

You will need to collect all your favorite photos or slides and organize them in the order you would like them to be presented or shown, such as chronological, subject, or family structure. If you wish to include titles, print them on the back of your slides or photos.

Choose carefully the pictures you would like to see at the beginning and the end of your video.

When choosing pictures, remember your television screen favors horizontal photographs. Vertical photos often require cropping and most likely will have filler bars on each side.

Music may also be included throughout the presentation. Choose your music carefully. Longer pieces of music work better. Most songs are approximately three minutes long. Video companies that make photomontages can pick out appropriate music if you find it difficult to choose.

To give you an idea of the length of a video presentation of your life story with music, here are some ideas:

❖ 99 pictures or less is approximately an 8-minute or less video with your choice of one or two songs or small sections of various songs.

❖ 100-140 pictures makes approximately an 11-minute or less video with about 3 songs or a portion of various songs.

❖ 140-180 pictures is approximately a 15-minute video with at least 3 full songs or a lot of portions of a variety of your favorite songs.

A photomontage of the story of your life is a beautiful gift to give to your friends and loved ones. While you are still alive you might enjoy watching your photomontage with the people closest to you. You may also want it shown at your memorial.

❖ Another way to use video may be to tape a final message to your friends and loved ones. Decide on a comfortable location that allows you to relax as you give your final words. If you have a tripod, you could self-record, or ask a loved one to record for you.

Special Messages and Presentations

So often, we have a family member or special friend whom we would like to honor. Your memorial or celebration of life presents a final chance to let them know how much they mean to you.

Take some time to write that special person/people a letter with words spoken from your heart. Then choose someone to read aloud your special thoughts during your memorial celebration.

If you find what you have written is too personal to be read in front of others, or you feel it is too long, then write it or type it on a nice piece of paper and place it in an envelope with the person's name on the outside. You may choose to put a ribbon around the envelope or decorate it in some way. You can designate a specific person to give your letter to the recipient.

Some people have special or meaningful jewelry, such as a wedding ring, necklace, or watch they would like to pass down to a family member or friend. If you have something special you would like to pass down to someone, write them a note telling them why the item is important to you and why you chose to give it to them. Then choose someone to present your gift and read your note aloud to this person during your memorial. Or you can have it given to them after your celebration, so as not to cause jealousy.

Another idea would be to have a beautiful wind chime purchased and have it presented to a friend or loved one. During its presentation, a lovely sentiment might be, "Whenever you hear the chimes blowing in the wind, know I am always with you and I love you."

Other items you may consider giving away are things from your favorite hobby, such as your golf clubs, fishing pole, a painting you made, a stamp or coin collection, your favorite book collection, or a quilt you made.

Your Eulogy

Your eulogy can be one of the most important aspects of your memorial or celebration of life, as it provides the opportunity for significant people in your life to honor you.

You can choose anyone you like to do your eulogy: a friend or family member, co-worker, teacher, clergy, doctor, someone you grew up with, or someone who is deeply touched by you.

You may want to ask several people to share vignettes of your life. Perhaps each one could focus on a particular aspect of your life: family, friends, work, social activities, organizations you belonged to, hobbies, or your faith.

Whomever you decide to do your eulogy, make sure they feel comfortable talking in front of people, especially under these circumstances.

There are so many aspects of your life's journey in your *Sacred Planner* it might be helpful for the person doing your eulogy to read through it.

After your eulogy, you may choose to have an open *Sharing of the Hearts,* which is explained on the next page.

Sharing of the Hearts

In your *Sacred Planner* you can mention you would like to have time available for whoever would like to spontaneously share their thoughts, feelings, or even stories about you and your life.

It's important for the people who want to participate in this way to be able to share from their hearts. As they tell stories about you, talk about your achievements, or share the profound difference you made in their lives, the healing process is allowed to begin.

Many times humor comes out through open sharing. It's a great cathartic feeling to be able to laugh at this time and share the joy you brought into their lives.

You might want to use candles as part of your presentation.

❖ Have a beautiful tray with sand in it. Allow your friends and loved ones to come up, briefly say a few words, then light a candle and place it in the sand, in honor of you. As the numbers of participants and candles increases, the glow from the candles becomes brilliant. This can bring about a feeling that your life will live on in the heart of your friends and loved ones.

Depending on where you choose to hold your memorial, you may need to have a microphone, but if it's a not in a large venue, you could use other things to spotlight the person who wants to share.

For example:

- ❖ If you enjoy baseball, you may choose to have a baseball tossed to the people who would like to share their thoughts and feelings.

- ❖ If you feel a connection to the Native American traditions, you may want to pass around a feather or rattle, and those who hold it will be honored as they speak.

- ❖ If your celebration is outdoors, you may gather everyone into a circle and pass around a flower, and when a person wants to share they will hold the flower until they have said all they desire.

If you choose to have an open sharing, decide what represents you, and let the stories unfold . . . as they will.

☙ ❧

Written from the Memories in their Hearts

Your friends and loved ones cherish many memories about your journey through life with them. You may want to give them an opportunity to express their thoughts and feelings in writing. After your guests have shared their memories, your loved ones will have another sacred keepsake and another part of you.

You may want a decorative book that represents you, where your guests can write down their memories. You can have blank pages for them to write whatever comes to mind, or you may want to have a few questions prepared in advance such as:

Your Name followed by:

❖ The quality I loved about you was . . .

❖ My favorite time together was . . .

❖ You made me laugh so hard when . . .

❖ I will never forget when . . .

❖ What I will miss most is . . .

❖ Together you and I were known for . . .

❖ What you taught me about life is . . .

❖ What I will always hold dear to my heart about you is . . .

The messages written will be cherished by friends, and loved ones.

Memorial Candle Ceremony

You might like to have a memorial candle ceremony held in your honor, or include this in your service.

You can request to have the candles placed in whatever way feels comfortable to you: in a circle, on top of a mantle, in a candelabra, or around your casket or urn.

You can choose one person or several people to light the candles. The following are examples:

Ceremony

❖ As we light these four candles in honor of you, we light one for our grief, one for our courage, one for our memories, and one for our love.

❖ The light from this candle represents our grief. The pain of losing you is intense. It reminds us of the depth of our love for you.

❖ The light from this candle represents our courage – to feel our sorrow, to comfort each other, and to change our lives.

❖ The light from this candle is in memory of you – the times we laughed, the times we cried, the times we were angry with each other, the funny things you did, and the caring and joy you gave us.

❖ The light from this candle is the light of love. A special place in our hearts will always be reserved for you. We thank you for the gift your life brought to each of us. We love you.

Another way to use a candle to symbolize your life might be:

❖ Arrange to have someone buy a large white candle, or your favorite colored one, and assign someone to light it at the beginning of your memorial. You may write down something like, "This candle represents my life and passing." After your ceremony, the same person or someone else can extinguish the candle and carry it out.

❧   ☙

A Gift to Attendees

There are endless possibilities for a give-away gift to your friends and loved ones who attend your final celebration of life.

First, begin by thinking of something that has special meaning to you.

❖   Perhaps you would like everyone to receive your favorite flower.

❖   You may choose one or more of your favorite poems and have them typed up in advance. You can place two poems side by side per page. You may want to put a decorative design on top of each poem. After your death, the only thing your friends or loved ones need to do is make copies of your poems, cut them down the center, roll them up and place a nice ribbon or bow around them. You may choose to use your favorite color for the ribbon or paper. If you have more than one poem, it might be nice to use different colored ribbon for each poem so people in attendance know there is more than one poem.

❖   Another idea is to choose your favorite flowers and have someone buy packages of your favorite flower seeds, some small flower peat pots, and good soil. Have the seeds and soil placed in a nice large container. When your memorial or celebration of life is over, have each person pick up their individual flower peat pot, and dip it into the communal pot of mixing soil and seeds. As they fill up their peat pot, have them say a private prayer or say a special thought to you. Then have everyone take their flower pot home, water the soil and seeds, and watch your favorite flower(s) grow in memory of you. You may want to have nice paper bags available for them to carry their peat pot home.

❖ If you are a chocoholic, maybe you would like to have a pretty bowl of Hershey Kisses or Godiva chocolates available for your friends and loved ones.

❖ If you are a golfer, you may want to have everyone receive a golf ball with your name engraved, or maybe a saying like "No Slice in the After Life." Or, if you loved to play the guitar, you might want to have guitar picks engraved with your name on them.

❖ Perhaps you want to have everyone receive a small bottle of bubbles, and request that whenever they are sad, you would like them to open up the bottle of bubbles and blow some into the wind. This can lighten things up for them.

❖ It might be nice to pass out a candle for everyone and perhaps have a picture of you glued onto the container that holds the candle.

❖ You could display a basket full of small assorted crystals (such as amethyst, tourmaline, clear quartz, different colored fluorite, or hematite for grounding) available for whomever wants one. Or, you could choose to have all rose quartz crystals and have someone announce to everyone that this crystal is for calming, opening up the heart, and love. Let them know when they are stressed they can rub the rose quartz crystal, and it can relax them as they think of you. Before you pass away, you can also put your energy into these crystals and say some prayers over them.

❖ You can write something special and have it printed on nice paper and passed out to everyone. Have a picture of you for everyone, and maybe even have your favorite poem printed on the reverse side of your photo.

❖ You may want to have a friend or loved one purchase a beautiful hanging plant such as a Creeping Charlie, Pothos, Spider Plant, or any of the Wandering Jew plants, and place it in a nice container. Then, when your memorial or celebration of life is over, have everyone pinch off a large hanging section of the plant and have your guests replant it at home. Any of these beautiful plants will grow without roots. They also thrive without a lot of care. As their plant grows and blossoms, it will remind them of you.

The possibilities of a give-away gift are endless. The question is what would be meaningful and represent you?

Scriptures

In the Appendix, you will find a selection of Bible Scriptures you may want to use at your memorial, celebration of life, releasing of your spirit, or your final resting place.

It is important to remember every translation of the Bible has different nuances in wording, so if you choose to have scriptures read, use the wording from a Bible that makes you feel comfortable.

There are other scriptures and meaningful verses the Jewish, Buddhist, and other faiths and religions might choose for their service which are not included in the Appendix.

Your Last Words

If you would like to write your last words, find a comfortable, tranquil environment where you can experience peace within your heart. Take a slow, deep breath and begin to write or record your last words to your friends and loved ones. This might be the greatest love letter you have ever written or spoken.

It doesn't matter if your message is short or long. What matters is you have an opportunity to share your final thoughts with those you love and appreciate in your life.

Would you like to honor someone with reading your last words aloud? If so, who would you like to read them? Write their name, phone number, and e-mail address in your *Sacred Planner*. Or, you could tape or video record your words and have them played at your memorial, celebration of life, reception, or final resting place.

It might be nice to have soft background music playing while your final words are shared with your friends and loved ones. If you choose to do this, what music would you like to use?

∂ℯ   ℯ∂

When Doves Fly –
Symbolic Releasing of Your Spirit

After your memorial or celebration of life, you may choose to have a symbolic releasing of your spirit. Some ideas are white doves, butterflies, bubbles, confetti, floating candles in a pond, fountain or pool.

If you choose to use doves or butterflies as the symbolic releasing of your spirit, look for this service through wedding companies as well as funeral services.

Throughout history, the dove has been a symbol of peace and deliverance. A dove release gives a sense of comfort to all those touched with the passage of your life. It brings calm, peace, and healing.

A single dove released is a personal tribute to you. It represents a sense of freedom, a sense of the releasing of your spirit. It radiates with the feeling and awareness you are at peace.

A twenty-one dove salute is when twenty or more doves accompany the single dove to join as escorts to guide the one on its journey home. The birds fly above your friends and loved ones in a breathtaking formation. This can be a heartfelt and symbolic conclusion to your memorial or celebration of life and is an awe-inspiring sight.

As the doves or butterflies are released, you might choose to have a song played, such as:

❖ Celine Dion, *Fly*

❖ Bette Midler, *Wind Beneath My Wings*

❖ Charley Pride, *Wings of a Dove*

Or you may want to have a poem read as the doves or butterflies are released. There are a couple appropriate poems in the Appendix for you to look over and consider.

If you decide to use a poem or song as part of your symbolic releasing of your spirit, write down in your *Sacred Planner* what you request.

Now that you have created a unique memorial honoring the story of your life, before you begin the next portion of your *Sacred Planner, Decisions You Must Make,* take a slow deep breath in through your nose. Now exhale, and let out a sigh. Take another slow deep breath in and hold it to the count of three. As you exhale, let go of any fears, tension or anxiety. Take another deep breath in and begin to feel a sense of calmness and warmth enter your being. This time as you exhale, let out a sound. Now it is time to answer some extremely important questions.

Chapter 3

Decisions You Must Make

☙   ❧

Vital Information

Your vital information will be helpful to your friends and loved ones, and some of the data will be needed upon your death to order your death certificate. A few of these questions you have answered before in your *Legacy of Love*. However, by responding briefly to the questions again, all of your vital information will be combined.

❖   Write down your complete legal name at birth and married name if it applies. Also include any AKA (Also Known As) names.

❖   What is your date and place of birth?

❖   What is your marital status?

❖   Where is your last place of residence? How many years have you lived there? What is the phone number?

❖   Write down the name, phone number, address, and e-mail address of the person who will be responsible for carrying out your memorial or sacred celebration of life. You may want to clarify the relationship you have with this person (spouse, significant other, friend, attorney, or executor).

❖   If you feel comfortable, it would be helpful to write your social security number and password to your computer. Only do so if you know this information will be kept in a secure location, such as a locked file cabinet. Also, include any combinations to any locks.

Your doctors and dentist will need to be notified, so include his or her names, phone numbers, addresses, and e-mail addresses. It would also be helpful to write down your health insurance company and your membership number.

In chapter 4 *"Information Needed Upon Your Death,"* there is a complete list of vital information that will be needed.

❧   ❧

Important People

There are numerous people you may want to ask to help with your final arrangements. Write down their name(s), phone number(s), and e-mail address(es).

- ❖ Who is the main person you have chosen to make sure all of your wishes are carried out?

- ❖ Upon your death, who would you like to notify your friends and loved ones?

- ❖ List the name of your executor or attorney, along with his or her phone number, address, and e-mail address.

- ❖ Write down who you have chosen to conduct your memorial service or celebration of life.

- ❖ Who would feel comfortable meeting with the funeral director and finalizing everything?

- ❖ Is there someone warmhearted and organized you would like to meet the out-of-town guests and arrange for their housing?

- ❖ Is there someone special you would like to greet your friends and loved ones at your memorial, celebration of life, or reception?

- ❖ Do you want to assign special ushers? If so, how many and who?

❖ Who will be in charge of making sure the reception is set up the way you desire?

❖ If need be, who would you like to make the necessary arrangements for the care of infants or minors?

❖ Who can maintain a list of your callers, flowers, and donations?

❖ Do you have a friend or loved one who has nice handwriting and is understanding? If so, you may want to have him or her answer the condolence letters and phone calls.

❖ If your executor is not going to be ordering your death certificates, who would you like to order them? How many copies will your executor need? List of possible requirements include social security, banking and financial institutions, brokerage firms, and real estate entities.

Legal Issues

Peace of mind is priceless, and when you have your legal affairs in order, your loved ones and you can have peace of mind.

Whether you are in optimum health or facing illness (*dis-ease*), it is important to have all your legal affairs in order. This will allow you to preserve your estate and to direct whether or not you wish to be put on life support.

Below is a brief description of the necessary legal documents you may want to get in order. You can go to the National American Bar Association website at <u>www.abanet.org/rppt/public</u> to find extended definitions and explanations. Each state has its own regulations and laws.

❖ A Power of Attorney is a written document signed by you giving another person power to act on your behalf to conduct your business. A Power of Attorney can be: a) general power of attorney, which covers all activities, or b) special power of attorney, which grants powers limited to specific matters such as selling a particular piece of real estate, handling some bank accounts, or executing a limited partnership agreement.

❖ A Living Will, also known as a Power of Attorney for Health Care or Advance Healthcare Directive, is a document authorized by statutes in all states in which you appoint someone as your proxy or representative to make decisions on maintaining extraordinary life support if you become too ill, are in a coma, or are certain to die soon. You can also state in your Living Will if there are people you do or do not want to have visit you.

❖ A Will is a written document which leaves your estate to your choice of any named persons or entities. If you don't have a will at the time of your death, your estate will pass by interstate succession according to the laws of the state where you die.

❖ A Trust is a legal entity which continues to exist after your death. Thus, property transferred to your trust before your death will pass according to your instructions in the trust without the need for probate. This can save a lot of time and expense, particularly if you own a home at the time of your death.

❖ Domestic Partners. If you are sharing the same residence with a person you consider to be your partner, there are some states, such as California, where there is a law that states surviving registered domestic partners will have all the rights of a surviving spouse following the death of their partner.

A registered domestic partnership may be established by two persons who are at least 18 years of age and a) both persons are members of the same sex or b) if the persons are of opposite sexes, at least one of them must be over age 62.

To establish a registered domestic partnership, the two persons must file a Declaration of Partnership with the Secretary of State. Merely living together doesn't create a domestic partnership.

Many members of the gay and lesbian community believe they have additional rights, including the right to control disposition; however, they can obtain these rights only by filing a Declaration of Partnership with the Secretary of State. For more information, please contact your Secretary of State department.

As you can see, it is critical you have your legal affairs in order. If you have a Power of Attorney, Will, Trust, Living Will, Power of Attorney for Health Care or Advance Healthcare Directive, include them with your Life Insurance Policy, Burial Insurance, and other important papers.

Write down the location of your legal documents. In your *Sacred Planner* it is also important to name your attorney or your executor and provide his or her phone number, address, and e-mail address.

❖ If you have children under the age of 18, it's extremely important to have your final affairs in order and state who you would like to be their legal guardian, upon your death, if no spouse.

❖ You may want to take the time to write an Ethical Will. This is not a legal document, but more like a personal letter. In your Ethical Will, you can share your values, blessings, life's lessons, hopes, and dreams for the future, as well as love and forgiveness with your family, friends, and community.

If you don't have your legal affairs in order, now might be the perfect time to do so.

Giving the Gift of Life

When you die or make your transition, you have an opportunity to save a life by donating your organs or tissues. What you donate could save the lives of 8 people and enhance the lives of more than 50 individuals, as you give them a second chance to experience the joys of life and living.

If you decide to be an organ or tissue donor, it is extremely important your loved ones know your wishes.

The manner in which a person dies determines the suitability of the organ or tissue donation. Organs can be donated from individuals who sustain an injury to the brain so severe the brain dies while the heart and body are being supported in an ICU. Tissues can be donated after the heart stops.

Lifesaving organs that can be donated include: heart, kidneys, lungs, pancreas, liver, and intestines. Tissues donated include: skin, tendons, bone, heart valves, veins, and corneas. Skin grafts can be used to treat the injuries sustained by burn victims; tendons and bones are used for rebuilding and supporting injuries; heart valves are used in place of mechanical valves; and veins can help revitalize areas of the body lacking blood supply. You can choose to donate all organs and tissues without compromising a viewing of your body at your memorial or celebration of life.

Medical professionals decide which organs and tissues are suitable for donation. You or your family member will be given the option of identifying the specific organs and tissues you wish to donate or taking the option of donating any organs and tissue suitable for transplantation. Additional options of donation for research or education are also encouraged.

If you choose to donate your entire body for medical research, you will need to arrange this with the medical school of your choice, well in advance. Each school has its own protocol and procedures that have to be followed. It's important to note there is no guarantee your body will be accepted as a donor. Some medical schools may not have an immediate need or provision for storage. Furthermore, the cause of death and condition of your body may render it inappropriate for medical education.

Some medical schools are responsible for the costs of your final disposition. The medical school will generally release the body or cremated remains to the family for burial anywhere from 6 months to 36 months after the date of death.

In some states, the Department of Motor Vehicles provides a donor card or access to a donor registry. If you choose to be a donor of any kind, make sure you sign and date your card and indicate what you want to donate or register with the donor registry. Also, if there is a sticker that comes with your DMV donor card, place it in the correct spot. Carry your donor card next to your driver's license or I.D. card. This will alert the appropriate authorities you want to be a donor. However, this may not be a guarantee you are a donor, because some states require verbal authorization from next of kin.

You will also want to have your request to be a donor written in your legal documents and in your *Sacred Planner*.

To access the requirements in your state, go to the Coalition of Donation website at www.donatelife.net and a map will appear. Click on the state you live in and it will give you the requirements and guidelines for your state.

The most important thing about being an organ or tissue donor is you have notified your loved ones of your wish to donate and what tissue or organ parts you want to give to another. Being a donor is a sacred gift of life you are giving since part of you will live on to enhance the lives of others.

Before the Removal of Your Body

Before the removal of your body, you may want your loved ones to perform a ritual, such as:

❖ Wash your body within two hours of your death

❖ Remove your clothing and place a drape over your body

❖ Dress and prepare your body

❖ Anoint your sacred body with oils

❖ Place candles around your body

❖ Burn incense

❖ Sound a bell or chime

❖ Read inspirational passages, scriptures, or poems

❖ Gather in prayer or silence

If you wear jewelry and glasses most of the time, have someone take them off before the removal of your body. Once your body is prepared for its resting place – in a casket or to be cremated – you may want to have some kind of jewelry buried or cremated with you. If so, decide who you would like to be responsible for making sure your jewelry or eyeglasses are placed on your body.

If you wear eyeglasses and do not plan on having them buried or cremated with your body, you may want to consider having them donated to an organization after your death. Your used glasses would be cleaned, repaired, classified by prescription, and then distributed worldwide to men, women, and children in need.

❖ Lions, Leos, and other volunteers collect used eyeglasses and sunglasses for donation to the Lions Eyeglass Recycling Centers which are located throughout the world. The following locations accept eyeglass donations as well: Lions collection boxes, Lions Eyeglass Recycling Centers, Offices of the American Optometric Association, the Canadian Association of Optometrist Members, and Goodwill Industry Stores. Consult your local directory for the location nearest you.

❖ Give the Gift of Sight^{SM} sponsored by Luxottica Group is another program that hand delivers recycled used eyewear to those in need in developing countries around the world. You can call Give the Gift of Sight^{SM} at 513-765-6000 in Mason, Ohio or log on to their website at www.givethegiftofsight .org to locate the nearest drop-off location for eyeglasses and sunglasses.

The Question of Embalming

Before you die, you can decide if you want to have your body embalmed. A lot of people are not aware they have a choice. Check with your local state laws to see if embalming is required. If your body is shipped to another location, it depends on the receiving state or country if your body needs to be embalmed.

True Muslims, Orthodox Jews, and certain other cultures or traditions do not permit embalming.

Mortuaries and funeral homes will allow immediate family members to view your body prior to being embalmed, as long as it is shortly after your death and not long before your public visitation/wake.

If you decide to have a home funeral, embalming is never required.

Your Remains

Have you decided if you want to be buried or cremated? Contemplating your death, and what you want done to your body after it dies, may be hard to think about, or you may find it liberating. Regardless of how you feel about it, death is an event we will all experience. It would be helpful to have an open conversation with your loved ones concerning your desires, and then write all your detailed wishes in your *Sacred Planner*.

It is your decision whether to be cremated or buried, however, your loved one(s) may oppose your choice. If your wishes are specified in legal documentation, your executor would have the legal obligation to carry out your wishes. This is why it's extremely important to have your wishes written down in your legal papers, and to make your wishes known to those closest to you.

Whether you choose to be buried or cremated, you can decide if you want a direct cremation or burial. In either case, there would not be a viewing of your body. Consider your loved ones before making your decision. If you decide on a direct cremation or burial with no viewing, it could be extremely hard on your family members, particularly those who may not be present during the time of your death. Some people may need that time of viewing to say goodbye. Seeing your body and the reality of your death allows your friends and loved ones to move towards the healing process. So when it comes to direct burial or cremation, think about those left behind before making your final decision.

If you decide to have a visitation/viewing of your body, would you like an open or closed casket?

Perhaps there is something important you would like to have buried or cremated with you such as a picture, rose bud heart wreath, poem, jewelry, or any religious items. If you decide to have something included in your burial or cremation, write a list of the items and where they are located.

The Federal Trade Commission has free information *"Funerals: A Consumer Guide"* with regulations concerning funerals and cemeteries. Their website is www.ftc.gov, and their toll free number is 877-382-4357.

Through the Cemetery and Funeral Bureau of the State Department of Consumer Affairs, you may obtain a free copy of *"Consumer Guide to Funeral and Cemetery Purchases,"* which will also be beneficial to read.

☙   ❧

Estimated Cost of Funerals

Your funeral could be one of the most expensive events in your life. Every mortuary, funeral home, and cemetery has their own price list, so ask them to mail you their complete packet of information and prices. If you decide to purchase your casket or urn from an independent dealer, make sure the company is reputable and meets the requirements of the cemetery.

To get an idea of the cost of funeral items, you can go onto the Internet and look over the information AARP has available. Their website is www.aarp.org/life/griefandloss. After you take the time to review the costs and your choices, you will be able to decide exactly what you want and how you want to be honored.

Your *Sacred Planner* will include all of your funeral information, but most importantly, it will include your unique wishes for your memorial service or celebration of life.

A Pre-Arranged Funeral

A pre-arranged funeral[4] arrangement allows you to pre-pay and carefully select all the necessary things you desire, such as your casket, urn, vault, cemetery property, marker, and flowers. You may also pay for the transportation of your loved ones, your hearse, flower van, police escort, clergy, and other things.

By planning ahead, you can decide if you want any special merchandise such as acknowledgment cards, prayer cards, a guest book, or religious items.

A carefully pre-planned funeral you have created by yourself or with the assistance of another, will be comforting to your family. While some families consider making funeral arrangements just another aspect of responsible estate planning, others see pre-arranged funerals as a very personal gift to loved ones. It offers the freedom from having to make important but distracting decisions at an otherwise difficult time.

Pre-arrangements through a mortuary or funeral home allows you to carefully select all your necessary items and lock them into today's prices, eliminating tomorrow's costs. By visiting the mortuary or funeral home of your choice, you have complete control of your funeral and all your preferences. Because of the timeframe between your pre-arrangements and funeral, the exact items you selected may not be available. However, the mortuary or

---

[4] The word *"funeral"* is used in the next few sections, because we are talking about mortuaries and cemetery items and *funeral* is the word they use.

funeral home will supply the style, quality, and value of the merchandise as close as possible to what you have selected.

❖ If you have already made arrangements with a mortuary, funeral home, or cemetery, write all the information in your *Sacred Planner*. State the exact location, contact names, e-mail addresses, and phone numbers of the people involved.

❖ If you haven't made arrangements at the mortuary, funeral home, or cemetery of your choice, you may want to think about doing it. This gives you the final say about your last wishes and relieves your loved ones of the burden of planning and paying for a funeral.

❖ If you don't feel comfortable going into a mortuary or funeral home, you may want to look at the National Funeral Directors Association's website at www.nfda.org where you will be able to read information and see various kinds of merchandise.

❖ If there comes a time you feel comfortable, take a friend or loved one and visit the mortuary or funeral home of your choice. Look through their merchandise and see their different chapels and waiting rooms.

The mortuary or funeral home will also offer to help you plan for the viewing of your body and a service, if you choose. The wonderful thing about your *Sacred Planner* is you have written all your desires, which can be used as a guide to carry out the way you want to be remembered and honored in your service.

Home Funerals

Until the time of the Civil War, home funerals were common. When a man, woman, or child passed away at home, loved ones came together to prepare the body before friends and family came to pay their final respects. They also dug a grave for the deceased and laid the body to rest near their home or in a natural setting.

In the United States, you can choose to have a home funeral. Caring for your loved ones who have died without a funeral director's involvement is currently legal in every state except Connecticut, Indiana, Louisiana, Nebraska, and New York. If you choose to have a home funeral, it's important to follow the state and local regulations, because the laws vary widely from state to state. For example, in some states you need a permit or medical permission to move a body. Following the death, the next of kin or an agent named in an Advanced Health Care Directive (AHCD) can act in lieu of a licensed funeral director and make all the arrangements and carry out your decisions.

Currently more people are looking into home funerals as an alternative to traditional funerals in mortuaries or funeral homes for a variety of reasons:

❖ Your loved ones have more control over the process and can participate as much or as little as they desire.

❖ Children can better understand death as a natural part of the cycle of life.

❖ Your loved ones can be involved with caring for your body.

❖ It can bring the family into the sacred rituals which make the death intimate.

❖ Friends and loved ones can create your casket or burial vessel.

❖ It's more natural, ecological, and affordable.

❖ Embalming is not required.

❖ Your family members can participate in your disposition.

There are committed people throughout the United States who are dedicated to educating families about the choices of caring for loved ones and bringing funeral rites back into the home. Their goal is to bring awareness about dying and death so people are more empowered when death occurs. These people want to allow the family to participate as much or as little as they desire and create a sense of community. This allows the family more time in their own personal way to process the death of their loved one, while it gives an aspect of empowerment and honors the rites of passage.

If you are interested in having a home funeral and would like to have your loved ones help prepare your body or home funeral, you may want to look at the following websites for more information about the classes and services offered at various locations.

❖ *Final Passages* started in 1995 by Jerrigrace Lyons and is located in Sebastopol, California. Their website is www.finalpassages.org and their phone number is 707-824-0268.

❖ *Sacred Crossings - Bringing Funerals Home* is located in Los Angeles, California. You can contact Olivia Bareham through their website at www.sacredcrossings.com or call 310-968-2763.

❖ For home funerals in Orange County, California, there are two women working together. You can contact Susan Wellborn at 714-964-0516, and Kathy Zutz at 714-556-8959.

❖ In San Diego, California, there is a licensed establishment called *Thresholds* that educates people about home funerals and will assist in the ceremony. You can contact Kat Alessi through their website at www.thresholds.us or call 619-358-9254.

❖ In Friday Harbor, Washington, there is *In Terre Funeral Rites.* You can contact Ciely Ti Gray at 360-378-6703 or visit their website at www.interrefuneralrites.com.

❖ In Boulder, Colorado, there is an organization called *Natural Transitions.* You can contact Karen Van Vuuren at 303-443-3418, or visit their website at www.naturaltransitions.org.

❖ In Boise, Idaho, helping you make choices for a family-directed funeral is *IdaHome Funerals.* Their website is www.idahomefunerals.com or you can contact Susan Randall at 208-830-4831.

❖ In Austin, Texas, you can contact Sandy Booth or Donna Belk at *Crossings Care Circle.* You can contact them through their website at www.crossingscircle.org or call them at 512-922-8043 or 512-440-7979.

❖ For a home funeral in the St. Paul, Minnesota area, there is an organization by the name of *Portages Alternative Funeral*

Advocacy and you can contact Jean Madsen and Michael Sorrell by e-mail at portagesafa@yahoo.com or you can call them at 651-398-8172. Their website is www.portagesafa.com.

❖ *Crossings: Caring for our Own at Death* is located in Takoma Park, Maryland. Contact Beth Knox at 301-523-3033 or through their website at www.crossings.net.

❖ *Final Journey Home* is located in Pittsburgh, Pennsylvania, and you can contact Rev. Lynn Acquafondata at 412-496-2445 or visit their website at www.finaljourneyhome.com.

❖ In Greensboro, North Carolina, there is an organization called *The Sophia Center for Life Studies.* You can contact Sandy LaGrega through e-mail at SunSan52@aol.com or call 336-292-7947. Sandy is associated with the Crossing Care Community.

❖ For more resources and services on home funerals, you can visit www.homefuneraldirectory.com.

PBS has a video documentary, "A Family Undertaking" created by Elizabeth Westrate that explores the complex psychological, cultural, legal, and financial issues surrounding home funerals. To obtain information about this video, go to www.pbs.org and in the search bar type in A Family Undertaking. When the site comes up, look for Elizabeth Westrate, which will be at the beginning .

For more information on home funerals or to verify if your state allows home funerals (since state laws change) you can call "Funeral Consumers Alliance" toll free at 800-765-0107 or visit their website at www.funerals.org.

If you would like to read about the necessary procedures and regulations, you will find the following books helpful:

❖ *Creating Home Funerals* by Jerrigrace Lyons (to obtain a copy contact "Final Passages" listed on page 78).

❖ *Living into Dying: Spiritual and Practical Care for Family and Community* by Nancy Poer.

❖ *Caring for the Dead: Your Final Act of Love* by Lisa Carlson.

❖ *The American Way of Death Revisited* by Jessica Mitford.

❖ *Grave Matters: A Journey Through the Modern Funeral Industry to a Natural Way of Burial* by Mark Harris.

❖ *Dealing Creatively with Death: A Manual on Death Education and Simple Burial* by Earnest Morgan.

❖ *Undertaken With Love: A Home Funeral Guide for Congregations and Communities.* You can purchase a copy at www.homefuneralmanual.org, or you can download a PDF copy for free. For questions please call Holly Stevens at 336-643-5947.

If you choose to have a home funeral, you may also be interested in having your remains placed in a natural burial site. Natural burial information is listed in the section, *"An Ecologically Responsible Choice,"* on page 83.

Your Garden of Eternity
The Cemetery

You may choose a corporate, county, private, national (military) cemetery, or natural memorial burial park for the burial of your remains. When selecting a cemetery property, take the time to walk or drive through the grounds. Does the cemetery incorporate things meaningful to you? Does it meet the requirements of your religion? Are there serene surroundings of natural beauty enhanced by fountains, monuments, and other features? On the other hand, maybe you like sweeping lawns combined with lakes and colorful gardens to complete an atmosphere of tranquility, solace, and everlasting peace. Allow yourself to get a feel for the different cemeteries, and then decide which one brings a feeling of inner peace and comfort.

Every cemetery has its own restrictions, regulations, and prices. If you have decided to have a burial of any kind, call around and compare the prices, locations, and amenities so you can make a wise decision on your final resting place.

It's also important to check with the cemetery of your choice to see if they allow monuments or only markers. In addition, will the cemetery allow you to have a permanent vase placed on your marker, if you choose? If so, ask if they allow artificial flowers or only fresh flowers. Some cemeteries allow you to have dual burials in one plot, which might appeal to your spouse or significant other.

❧   ❧

An Ecologically Responsible Choice

There's a growing desire among environmentally conscious individuals to be buried in a Memorial Nature Preserve. In Great Britain, there are over 200 green cemeteries for natural burials. For thousands of years families had "Green Burials," and only in the past century have we strayed away from it. But the idea is beginning to catch on again in the United States.

The goal of Memorial Nature Preserves in the United States is land preservation and restoration. The staff is conscious of preserving nature, and the people look at the natural history of the location. At these preserves, there's an exchange; being a community within nature, you have to give back by becoming part of nature again. Saving the land bonds people with nature.

Burials are not the dominant reasons for these nature preserves, which serve as multidimensional social spaces for picnics, weddings, burials, education, art, photography, scientific research, and much more. Rituals are common because the people see rituals as a door to transformation.

The Memorial Nature Preserves are a convenient, economical, beautiful, environmentally responsible, and mainstream alternative to existing memorial parks. They represent an ecologically sustainable way to be buried. There's less pollution than with cremation, and the preserves do not waste valuable land.

Burial and ashes scatterings or placement occur in Memorial Nature Preserves, but the burial must be natural, "dust to dust" burials; no toxic embalming fluids, no vaults, and only biodegradable caskets are allowed. The graves are marked only in natural ways, with a planting of a tree or shrub, or the placement of a flat indigenous stone. Because these things are natural, the total funeral costs for burial are much less expensive than at traditional cemeteries.

Your family and loved ones can partake in making your casket and digging your grave if they wish. With the burial in a natural environment, loved ones may hear birds singing, water trickling, and leaves blowing in the wind as they lower your casket into the ground (if they choose) and sprinkle dirt upon your casket.

Memorial Nature Preserves represent a place of continuation and solace, where your friends and loved ones can walk and remember you. This is also a way of being remembered by creating a sense of permanence in the form of a forest, meadow, or field, and doing something to help Mother Earth.

Currently in the United States, there are several Memorial Nature Preserves but more are in development. If you are interested in this type of burial, or you would like to visit these beautiful environments, go to the following websites for more information:

- ❖ Ramsey Creek in South Carolina, the first Memorial Nature Preserve, opened in 1998. You can contact Billy or Kimberley Campbell at 864-647-7798 or visit their website at www.memorialecosystems.com. At Ramsey Creek, you are allowed to have a ground shroud burial instead of a biodegradable casket.

- ❖ In Glendale Florida, there is the Memorial Nature Preserve. You can contact them through their website at www. glendalenaturepreserve.org or call 850-859-2141.

- ❖ In Mill Valley, California, there is Fernwood. Their phone number is 415-383-7100 and their website is www. foreverfernwood.com.

- ❖ There are over 300 providers in United States who are conscious about green burials. The Green Burial Council has cemetery operators in many states who are willing to accommodate green burials, as well as funeral professionals who can provide services/products that do not involve the use of toxins or materials that are not biodegradable. You can contact Joe Sehhe at the Green Burial Council at 888-966-3330 or visit their website at www.greenburial.org, to find a provider near you.

- ❖ When you go on the Internet and type the words *natural burials* into a search engine, you'll find an informative site, Living Legacies, at www.livinglegacies.co.nz. This organization is located in Motueka, New Zealand and their phone number is 03-528-5220.

You can also obtain more information from the following websites:

- ❖ The North American Woodland Burial Society is an information exchange. You can visit them at www.woodlandburial .htmlplanet.com.

- ❖ In Canada, the Memorial Society of British Columbia's website is www.memorialsocietybc.org and their phone number is 888-816-5902.

If you are interested in a natural burial, you may also be interested in the information in the section, *"Home Funerals,"* on page 77.

෩   ෨

Military Funeral and Honors

If you are a military veteran, you may choose to have your remains placed in a National (Military) Cemetery. The government will pay for your burial and a government headstone or marker, but not your casket, container, or any additional items. Niche markers are also available to mark columbaria used for inurnment or cremated remains. Be sure your loved ones have access to your discharge papers (DD214) when making the necessary arrangements for your Military Funeral Honors.

The following are eligible for Military Funeral Honors:

❖ Military members on active duty or Selected Reserve.

❖ Former military members who served on active duty and departed under conditions other than dishonorable.

❖ Former military members who completed at least one term of enlistment or period of initial obligated service in the Selected Reserve and departed under conditions other than dishonorable.

❖ Former military members discharged from the Selected Reserve due to a disability incurred or aggravated in the line of duty.

Most National (Military) Cemeteries have a chapel available for a service or gathering of your choice. You may have someone you know personally present your memorial service. Initially, the United States flag and perhaps your military cap will be placed on top of your casket (when applicable). A formal ceremony will be performed by an Honor Guard detail consisting of not less than two members of the Armed Forces. One member of the detail will be a representative of your parent service. The honor detail will, at a minimum, perform a ceremony that includes the folding and presenting of the American flag to your next of kin and the playing of *Taps*. *Taps* will be played by a bugler, if available, or by electronic recording. Today, there are so few buglers available that the Military Services often cannot provide one.

If you have served as an officer in the military for 20 years or more, you will be honored with a 21-gun salute.

Who would you like to receive the American flag and the spent gun shells?

If your husband or wife chooses to be buried in the military cemetery next to you or with you, the mortuary will need a copy of the marriage certificate in order to process the request. The cost of having your spouse buried in the military cemetery is extremely low or free.

For more information about a Military Funeral Honors or to obtain a copy of your discharge documents, contact the National Personnel Records Center or access the information via the Internet at www.archieves.gov/verterans/evetrecs/index.

On the Internet type in "Military Honors" into a search engine. The first site will be Military Funeral Honors home page, sponsored by the Department of Defense. You will find frequently asked questions, a standard form 180 questionnaire, related links, and much more.

For information regarding burials in the Department of Veterans Affairs National Cemeteries, go to www.cem.va.gov. This website has links to related sites such as how to obtain a Presidential Memorial Certificate (41A1C). Arlington National Cemetery is under the jurisdiction of the Department of the Army and their telephone number is 703-607-8585.

The Veteran's Administration toll-free phone number is 800-827-1000, or you can go to www.va.gov.

You can also call the following numbers direct for information on Military Honors: Air Force 800-531-5803; Army 800-626-3317; Coast Guard 877-645-4667; Marine Corps 800-847-1597; Navy 800-368-3202.

Military Honors Burial-at-Sea Ceremony

The Department of the Navy offers a Military Honors burial-at-sea ceremony to the following:

- ❖ Active duty members of the United States uniform services and their dependents.

- ❖ Retired members of the United States uniform services and their spouse if not divorced.

- ❖ Former members of the United States uniform services discharged under honorable conditions and their spouse if not divorced.

- ❖ United States civilian marine personnel of the Military Sealift Command.

- ❖ Other United States citizens who are determined eligible for at-sea committal due to notable service or outstanding contribution to the United States. The Office of Naval Operations must approve these cases.

The Navy ports that carry out Military Honors burial-at-sea in the United States are: Honolulu, Hawaii; San Diego, California; Bremerton, Washington; Corpus Christi, Texas; Portsmouth, Virginia; and Jacksonville, Florida.

For casket burials, your casket must be metal. The mortuary will hold your body until the ship is ready to deploy. Some mortuaries require a refrigeration fee until the deployment. Because your body will be held until the ship deploys, your body must be embalmed and preserved before departure of the Navy vessel.

The Military Honors burial-at-sea will be performed once a Navy ship is deployed on official business. Therefore, your loved ones would not be present for your ceremony.

Once the ship has united 10 deceased people of the same religious preference, and the ship is ready to deploy, the Commanding Officer can perform your Military Honors burial-at-sea ceremony. The ship has to reach a depth greater than 600 feet (100 fathoms) before the Commanding Officer of the ship is authorized to perform the military service.

If you are going to be cremated, your ashes will be carried aboard the Navy ship in an urn or container and your ashes can be scattered or placed off an aircraft, plane, helicopter, fleet, or submarine.

The Commanding Officer will notify your family by letter about the date and time of your service and include a nautical chart with the longitude and latitude of your Military Honors burial-at-sea ceremony. Your family will also receive three spent gun shells.

Each Commanding Officer does things differently, but you can request your family send a blank VHS tape or a disposable camera for a videotape or photos of your Military Honors burial-at-sea ceremony. Aircrafts, however, cannot videotape.

For complete information on Military Honors burial-at-sea ceremonies go to www.history.navy.mil/faqs/faq85-1.htm.

For more information about a Military Honor funeral or to obtain a copy of your discharge documents, contact the National Personnel Records Center or access the information via the Internet at <u>www.archives.gov/veterans/evertrecs/index</u>.

On the Internet type "Military Honors" into a search engine. The first site will be Military Funeral Honors home page, sponsored by the Department of Defense. There you will find frequently asked questions, standard form 180 questionnaire, related links and much more.

The Veteran's Administration toll-free phone number is 800-827-1000, or you can go to <u>www.va.gov</u>.

Your Attire

If you knew tomorrow would be the last day of your life, what outfit would you pick to wear for your final farewell? Think about what makes you feel good. Is it something comfortable, classy, stylish, casual, or maybe even a sports uniform? On the other hand, maybe you would feel honored wearing your military uniform. Perhaps you would like to wear an outfit in your favorite color. Don't forget to accessorize with your favorite jewelry.

Pick whatever you would like to wear for your final appearance, be it burial or cremation. Many times, under stress, family members or loved ones will argue over the little things, such as what the deceased person should be wearing when buried or cremated. Keep the peace and state exactly how you would like to look on your final day.

Then decide if you want to be buried or cremated with any jewelry or glasses on. If not, who do you want to be responsible for removing them from your body?

Do you have a favorite hair stylist or makeup artist you would like to apply your cosmetics? If so, be sure to include their name, phone number and e-mail address in your *Sacred Planner*. Also, make sure you talk to your stylist in advance to see if he or she would be comfortable performing this service.

Mortuaries and funeral homes have trained people to do hair and makeup. If you choose to have them assign someone to do your makeup and hair, they will need several pictures of you so they can make you look natural.

❧   ❧

Now I Lay Me Down to Rest

The purpose of the casket is for transportation of the body. There's a large selection of casket materials such as steel, copper, stainless steel, bronze, concrete, and wooden in a variety of exterior materials and interior finishes from which to choose. Caskets can also be personalized to reflect your hobbies or interests. Your friends and loved ones may want to get together and build a home-made casket, if you decide to be buried in a Memorial Nature Preserve.

You can see various types of caskets and liners by visiting mortuaries, funeral homes, or their websites, or by going onto the Internet type *caskets, funeral merchandise,* or *funerals* into a search engine to get some ideas. You may also purchase a casket through dependable retail stores.

You will need to decide if you want to have an open or closed casket during any type of ceremony. Make sure you include your choice in your *Sacred Planner*.

Think about who you would like to honor you as your pallbearers. Usually you would assign 6 to 8 people (male or female) to be your pallbearers. Once you have chosen them, list their names, phone numbers, e-mail addresses, and their relationship to you in your *Sacred Planner*.

If your casket is pre-paid, write down the business or company name, location, contact person, phone number and e-mail address. Because of the timeframe between when you purchased your casket and your funeral, the exact items you selected may not be available. However, the mortuary or funeral home will supply the style, quality, and value of the merchandise as close as possible to what you have selected.

❧   ❦

Ashes to Ashes, Dust to Dust

If you decide on cremation, you can choose the type of container for your ashes. Your ashes can be presented in a variety of types and styles of containers such as bronze, marble, wood, classic cloisonné, flag cases, angels, book ends, glass handcrafted vases, or jewelry. You can also have your urn personalized through engraving or the use of brass plaques.

Plastic containers often called "utility" or "temporary" urns are not permanently sealed and therefore are easy to reopen. This type of urn generally is used to carry your ashes to the location where you would like them to be scattered or placed.

You can see various types of urns by visiting the mortuary or funeral home of your choice or their website. Or you can type *urn,* or *funeral merchandise* into a search engine to get some ideas.

Decide how you would like to have your ashes dispersed. Some examples might be: placed in the cemetery in a columbarium niche, scattered or placed at sea, scattered or placed in the forest, placed in a loved one's garden, or displayed in an urn. Make sure you have authorization, before hand, if you want your ashes scattered or placed on private property. Permission is not required to scatter or place your ashes in waterways. However, check with your local or regulatory entity for the correct distance from the shoreline.

If you choose to have your ashes scattered or placed in a remote area on land or in water, remember this prevents your family and loved ones from making visits to your final resting place and will not allow them to place a permanent memorial at your site.

If you decide to have your ashes scattered or placed at sea, you may want to have the longitude and latitude known for the comfort of your loved ones.

❖ If you are a scuba diver or feel a connection to the ocean life, there's a company called Eternal Reefs, which can create a permanent living legacy using your remains. Your loved ones can bring your ashes (or mail them) to their location in Sarasota, Florida. Your loved ones can help mix your ashes into a concrete reef mold with holes in it for fish to swim in and out, creating a new habitat for fish and other marine life. Once the mold is hard, Eternal Reefs will place a plaque with your name and any message you would like engraved. When this is complete, they will place your reef in the ocean. Your loved ones can go out on the boat to witness the anchoring of your reef. They will also receive a letter indicating the longitude and latitude of your reef. Cementing your remains in a reef not only preserves a permanent living legacy in your name, but also helps sustain ocean life.

Eternal Reefs anchor reefs off the coast of Florida, South Carolina, North Carolina, Maryland, New Jersey, and Texas. You can contact Eternal Reefs at 888-423-7333 or visit their website at www.eternalreefs.com.

❖ Some people have chosen to have their ashes mixed with pottery clay and made into pots, cups, rocks, or stepping stones for their loved ones.

If you choose to have your ashes scattered or placed anywhere, state in your *Sacred Planner* who you would like to place or scatter them. This can be an extremely sacred experience for him or her and a real honor as well.

If there is anything special you would like during the scattering or placement of your ashes, such as last words from you or someone else, a song, poem, prayer, or anything else, write down those wishes.

Call the companies of your choice and get their prices and brochures relative to the different services. Find out who can transport your ashes to your favorite resting place or location. Place the company brochure of your choice in the back of your *Sacred Planner*. Example: If you want to have your ashes scattered or placed out at sea, find out what motorboats and sailboat companies perform sea burials, then make your decision and place their brochure in the back of your *Sacred Planner*.

There are endless possibilities regarding your burial or cremation. The important thing is to think about what resonates with you. What brings you joy, happiness, and peace?

~ ~

Saying the Last Goodbyes
Visitation - Wake

A visitation, also known as "the wake," is the time your friends and loved ones spend time with your body. Usually your family will view your body for the first time in privacy. You may choose to have your visitation at the mortuary, funeral home, church, a private residence, or other locations.

Many people believe when the physical body dies the spirit lives on, so they may not feel the need for a viewing of a body. Yet for some it's important to have an opportunity to spend time with your physical body for the last time. By doing so, they will come to terms with the reality of your death. Perhaps once they experience closure with your physical body, they will be able to be in touch with your spirit.

A visitation is a personal and cultural choice and usually takes place a day or two before your memorial or celebration of life. Traditionally the Jewish faith does not view the body.

❖ If you choose to have a visitation, you need to decide if you want to have your casket open or closed and where you would like this to take place, such as the mortuary, funeral home, a loved one's home, parish, temple, club, or organization.

❖ If you decide to have a wake, think of anything special you may like, such as your favorite music played, your favorite mementos displayed, candles or incense burned, bells rung, a special arrangement of flowers, or a guest book.

❖ If you choose to have a visitation before your body is cremated, you can rent a casket that has an individual removable lining, or purchase a special casket designed for cremation.

Going Out in Style

When you look back and remember special occasions such as weddings, Bar Mitzvahs, birthdays, or anniversaries, there's usually a theme played out which represents the person(s) being honored. Why not take time to plan a themed memorial and go out in style? Some mortuaries and funeral homes today are helping people create unique memorials which truly represent the person's life.

❖ In St. Louis, Missouri, the Wade Funeral Home offers a variety of themed visitation rooms.

Their first one was designed in 2002 and is the *"Traditional Vignette,"* set up like a 1940s parlor. It goes back to the times when loved ones brought the deceased family member's body back home for a viewing or for a home funeral. The 1940s parlor walls are decorated with old-fashioned wallpaper and backboards with windows. Outside one of the windows is a mural with a breathtaking outdoor scene. The glossy hardwood floors have scattered throw rugs throughout. There's a sitting room with an old-fashioned table lamp and telephone. At the head of the casket is a love seat and ottoman, and at the foot of the casket is a table with a mirror and flowers. In front of it is another table for your loved ones to place personal mementos. There are two antique chairs and a "what not" shelf on which to have your personal knickknacks placed. In the parlor, there's a piano available for your loved ones to play your favorite music.

In their *"Big Mama's Kitchen"* vignette, your friends and loved ones can gather in the kitchen setting which has a 1950s stove complete with a Crisco can for drippings, a sink, and refrigerator. On top of the stove are pots filled with dry ice which creates the appearance of something steaming in the pots. The cupboards are filled with Mama's pots and pans, and in the oven is a baked (fake) pie with an air freshener of "Grandma's cookies." The dinette table has a heaping platter of real fried chicken, and the smell filters throughout the setting. The table is set for whatever time of day the visitation will take place. In the morning, there might be real-looking pancakes, eggs, orange juice, and coffee. In the later part of the day, you might find steak, potatoes, and all the trimmings that go along with the meal.

Wade's also has a *"Sports Junkie"* view room with a La-Z-Boy recliner chair and a remote control television, where footage of your favorite basketball or football team can be played. The walls are decorated with posters from your favorite sporting activity. If you enjoyed fishing, there's a pond stocked with live fish, and sitting next to the pond are fishing poles, a tackle box, and lawn chair. All your loved ones need to do is add in your own personal things.

Wade Funeral Home in St. Louis, Missouri will create a personal vignette. You can call them at 314-385-4800, or visit their website at www.wadefuneralhome.com.

❖ In Las Vegas at any of the Palm Mortuaries, you can arrange your memorial using a variety of their props and set designs, plus your own personal items. If you enjoy golf you may be interested in *"The 19th Hole"* which has backdrop scenery of a golf course, two large irons 7-8 feet tall, and a golf bag filled with floral bouquets made to look like golf balls. You could be dressed in your favorite golf outfit and tuck your 3-wood in your casket. As a final touch, any of your trophies or photos of you on the fairway could surround you.

You can contact Palm Mortuary in Las Vegas, Nevada through their website at www.palmmortuary.com or call them at 702-464-8500.

If you're interested in having a unique visitation, there may be a place located near you that offers them. If not, you can still choose a theme by including your special mementos, such as paintings you did, quilts you made, your Harley Davidson, your dance shoes, your golf clubs, favorite pictures, and trophies. Display things that represent you.

❖ Here is an example of a celebration I assisted a man named George to create. After I videotaped his life story, we were able to create a unique memorial. He loves to golf, so he called his private country club to see if when he dies he could have his celebration on the greens. They agreed, so George wrote down that he wants to have his memorial at sunset on the 1st tee. He plans to have photos of him and his golfing friends, his trophies, shoes, clubs, and attire.

He wants to give his closest friend, Jim, his bag and clubs, so George wrote a personal note (for someone else to read aloud) stating, "Jim, you've never experienced the thrill of making a par, so I'm giving you my clubs and look forward to watching you make your first par."

As a give-away gift to everyone, George is going to have golf balls engraved with his name on one side, and on the other side *"No Slice in The After Life."*

Dinner will be at the country club with an open menu and will be fully paid for with all the alcohol included. George knows his friends and loved ones will have a fun time laughing and telling stories as they celebrate his life.

Your Final Drive
The Procession (Motorcade)

The procession, which is sometimes referred to as "the motorcade," is the orderly transportation for your loved ones to arrive at your final resting place. It is a symbol of mutual support and the public honoring of your death. The procession is led by your funeral (motor) coach and followed by your family and friends. Your state may require you have a police escort for your procession. Verify if police escorts are needed, and if so, how many police officers are required. The mortuary or funeral home of your choice should have this information available for you.

You may choose to have the procession drive past locations meaningful to you such as your home, your place of employment, or a favorite location where you spent a lot of time (country club, beach). If you would like your friends and loved ones to drive by your special places one last time with you leading the way, make sure you make it known in your *Sacred Planner*.

When deciding on a procession, you may also want to pre-pay for the use of additional limousines for the comfort of your loved ones. The mortuary or funeral home can arrange this.

❧　☙

Going Back to the Earth
Gravesite

At your final resting place, do you want a gathering? If so, do you want a private family or public community gathering? There are a couple of ways to have your casket presented: partially lowered where the top of the casket is at ground level or not lowered until your loved ones leave the cemetery. Is there a special way you would like your casket presented?

If you choose to have a gravesite gathering, is there anyone special you would like to lead the service or gathering? If so, ask that person if they will do the honors, and then write down their name, e-mail address, and phone number.

Would you like to have the flowers from your memorial or celebration of life brought to your final resting place?

Some traditions are carried out at the gravesite. For a Roman Catholic, the priest will sprinkle holy water over the casket and ground, symbolizing the consecration of the grave. Some Christians sprinkle sand over the casket as a symbol of the phrase "earth to earth, ashes to ashes, and dust to dust." At a traditional Jewish graveside service, when the casket is lowered to the bottom of the grave, a loved one will shovel earth over the casket. Is there anything special you would like?

Think about the final moments your friends and loved ones will have.

❖ Maybe you would like to have everyone hold hands in a circle around your gravesite.

❖ How about having some music played, friends singing your favorite song(s), or someone playing an instrument such as a sax, flute, fiddle, harp, guitar, or bagpipes?

❖ You may want to have your favorite poem read or have a flag blowing in the wind.

Do you want everyone to remain at your gravesite until your casket is lowered into the ground? If so, you may choose to have your friends and loved ones put something symbolic on top of your casket as it is lowered, such as flowers, pebbles, a handful of dirt, or sand.

As a tribute to your life, you may want a symbolic releasing of your spirit with doves or butterflies. If you decide to do this, several songs and poems that might be beneficial for the releasing of your spirit are listed in the section, *"When Doves Fly: Symbolic Releasing of Your Spirit,"* on page 53.

After you have been buried, your monument or marker will be placed within a short time. Take time to think about what you would like inscribed on your monument or marker. Also, decide if you would like to have a permanent flower vase installed.

It's important to check with the cemetery of your choice to find out their rules and regulations.

Time to Eat, Drink, and Tell Stories
Reception

The reception is an informal time for family to thank friends who shared in your memorial ritual. This is a time to offer condolence and mutual support and to begin the transition of life after death for those left behind.

The reception can take place right after your memorial service or after your remains have been put to rest.

If you decide to have a reception, you can decide to have it anywhere you desire, so why not pick a place that has special meaning to you?

❖ If you prefer an indoor setting, it could be held at a private residence, township hall, casino, university center, museum, a club, or the mortuary.

❖ On the other hand, perhaps you would like the reception scheduled for outside (weather permitting) at a public park, on the beach, on a boat, in the forest, or out in the desert.

You can decide the location and set the tone of your reception.

Would you like to have any of the flowers from your memorial or celebration of life brought to the reception? If there are any special mementos you would like displayed, music or songs played, or your favorite food available, indicate your wishes in your *Sacred Planner*.

Announcing Your Transition
Your Obituary

When it comes to your obituary, just thinking about writing it may cause some anxiety, or you may feel a sense of joy that you get to write your last words. If you choose to write your own obituary, start by thinking of it as a small biography. Look through your local newspaper under the Death, Funeral, and the Obituary section for ideas.

❖ You may keep your obituary simple and just state your name, age, date of death, your survivors, and where and when the service will be held.

❖ You may choose to make your obituary more personal by including your date and place of birth, titles, achievements, organizations, major places you lived, occupation, names of your loved ones who have gone before you, and your surviving family members and where they live (city, state, and country only). If you were in the military, you might want to add your branch of service you were in, where you were stationed, and if you were in any wars and received any medals. You could also request that donations are sent to your favorite organization in your name. Mention in your *Sacred Planner* if you want your age and cause of death included. For example: "At the age of XX, (your name) passed on peacefully at home due to (state illness)." You might want to include a poem or short phrase.

❖ If you're going to have a viewing/visitation or memorial service listed in the paper, don't publish anywhere publicly where your reception gathering will be held. Unfortunately, some individuals prey on those who are suffering and might break into your home during your reception. Have someone announce at your memorial or celebration of life where the reception will take place and have maps available to the location site.

❖ In addition to your local newspaper, you may wish to place your obituary in the newsletters of the clubs or organizations to which you belonged, or in your community church or congregation announcements.

❖ If you traveled to certain locations often or have an out-of-town get-away place where you are known, you may want to have your obituary published in their local paper as well.

❖ For your friends or loved ones who may not be able to attend your final celebration, check with the mortuary or funeral home to see if they have an online message or condolence guest book. If so, make that known in your *Sacred Planner*.

❖ The Internet has become an instant source of communication, and because of this, you may choose to have your obituary placed on the Internet. Most mortuaries and funeral homes have an online means of doing this for you. Your tribute on the Internet will be viewed worldwide for a period of time.

Flowers or Charity?

At your visitation, memorial, celebration of life, or final resting place, would you like to have some of your favorite flowers displayed? If so, indicate what kind of flowers. You may want to type *funeral flowers* into a search engine to see the different arrangements available. You'll find casket sprays, hearts, crosses, baskets, wreaths, inside pieces, bouquets, and other items. You can decide how elaborate you want your flower display to be.

You may wish to arrange for a few special floral bouquets at your memorial, and then request in lieu of sending flowers, your friends and loved ones send donations to your favorite organization, charity, or foundation in remembrance of your life. A donation to your favorite organization or charity adds another layer of meaning to your life by encouraging friends and loved ones to help others through your death.

If you choose to have donations sent to your favorite organizations, charities, or foundations, be sure to write down their names, addresses, and e-mail addresses.

❧   ❧

Remembrance
Your Life After Death

On the first or any anniversary date of your death, your friends and loved ones may wish to honor you. You may suggest the following ways to do so:

❖ Make another donation to your favorite charity or organization.

❖ Have a mass, service, or ritual said in your name.

❖ Purchase an item such as a tree and have it planted in honor of your life.

❖ If your memorial or celebration of life was at a picturesque location, such as a park, a beautiful chapel, or near the bay, your loved ones may want to revisit the site.

❖ They may choose to light a candle and do a ritual.

❖ Have a gathering or party and share stories of your times together.

❖ A loved one may want to set up a scholarship fund in honor of you.

In the section, *"A Dedication in Your Name,"* on page 34, you'll find ideas that might help your friends and loved ones find a way to celebrate the remembrance of your life and any anniversary of your death. Share these ideas in your *Sacred Planner* for your friends and loved ones to discover.

❧ ❧

Chapter 4

Important Information Needed Upon Your Death

Information Needed For Your Death Certificate

The following will be needed to order your certificate of death:

❖ Your given first name

❖ Middle name

❖ Your last (family) name

❖ AKA, Also Known As – include full AKA (first, middle, last)

❖ Date of birth mm/dd/yyyy

❖ Age

❖ Sex

❖ Birth state/country

❖ Social security number

❖ Ever in U.S. Armed Forces

❖ Marital status (at time of death)

❖ Education – Highest level/degree

❖ Race

❖ Usual occupation – type of work for most of your life. DO NOT USE "RETIRED."

❖ Kind of business or industry (such as grocery store, road construction, airline, employment agency)

❖ Years in occupation

❖ Your residence – street and number or location

❖ City, county, province, zip code

❖ Years in county

❖ State, country

❖ Informant's name, relationship (the person who provides information in this section).

❖ Informant's mailing address (street and number or rural route number, city or town, state and zip code)

❖ Name of your spouse – first, middle, last (maiden name)

❖ Name of father – first, middle, last, birth state

❖ Name of mother – first, middle, last (maiden), birth state

❧   ❧

Taking Your Final Breath Abroad If You Die Outside of the United States

If you are a person who loves to travel for pleasure or travels a lot for business, you might want to think about this. If you were to die outside of your state or country, where would you like your remains shipped?

If you die outside the United States, a friend or loved one should contact the local mortuary or funeral home in the city, town, and state where you want your final resting place. The mortuary or funeral home will make the necessary arrangements to have your remains shipped back.

Regardless of your citizenship, when you die outside of your country, your death must be registered in the country in which your death occurred.

Each country has its own regulations as to what kind of container or casket can be shipped out of their country. Your local mortuary or funeral home will know the country's rules and regulations. Once all your paperwork is in order, the mortuary or funeral home will make the arrangements with the airline company that will be transporting your remains back into the United States.

The cost for shipping your remains will vary depending on the country and where your remains will be shipped from and to, and what kind of container or casket is used. Your loved one may also choose to have your remains shipped back to the United States through FedEx or another worldwide company.

There won't be an entry fee or paper work. All the airlines will need is an airway bill (which includes your proper documents) on your casket or container. This is under Section 8 General 8 of the airline regulations.

If you're a traveler, bring peace of mind to you and your loved ones by mentioning in your *Sacred Planner* the town or city and state where you would want your remains shipped.

Taking One More Flight - Carrying Ashes on Airlines in the United States

If a friend or loved one wants to transport your ashes in an urn or another type of container from one location to another via the airlines, he or she can legally carry your ashes on board. Your friend would go to the security check point and ask to speak to the supervisor. The supervisor will not open the urn or container, but will place something metal, like a belt buckle on the top, bottom, or side of your urn or container. If the X-ray machine and the security person/screener can see the metal item through the container, they will allow your loved one to carry your ashes on board the plane.

If the security supervisor can't see through the container by using a metal item, security will be required to have the container or urn with your ashes sent to baggage cargo where it will receive special handling.

❧　☙

Chapter 5

Sharon's Near-Death Experience

(NDE)

Given the Choice to Live or Die
My Near-Death Experience (NDE)
March 1997

Death is a chapter in life few people are comfortable talking about. But sometimes in life we are given a glimpse of that final corporeal life chapter and even given a choice whether to stay or go beyond. I was blessed with such an experience. Like many people facing death, I was too sick to talk about dying and how I wanted my life to be celebrated. In addition, like many loved ones of an ill person, my family found it difficult to talk about me dying.

As you read my near-death experience and travel with me through the Tunnel of Light, you may be able to understand the beauty and sacredness of our life and death. Every person has their own connection to what holds true to their spirit, their soul, and their heart. Throughout this chapter I use the names *God* and *Infinite Spirit,* as two of the many names I call my source of life and the Creator of all. There are hundreds of names you can replace for *God* and *Infinite Spirit* such as: Lord, Almighty, Supreme Being, Deity, Creator, Godhead, Omnipotent, Omniscient, All Merciful, Higher Power, Divine, Tao, Holy One, Allah, Elohim, Yahweh, Kadosh, I Am, the Alpha and Omega, and Life Giver. As you read through this chapter, when I use the name *God* or *Infinite Spirit*, replace it with whatever name resonates with you.

An exercise for you...

Gently close your eyes. Breathing through your nose, take a slow deep breath in, then exhale and let out a sigh. Take another slow deep breath, and as you exhale let go of any fears, tension, or anxiety. Take another deep breath and begin to feel a sense of calmness, inner peace, and warmth enter your Being.

Become aware of your heartbeat. Now tap into the rhythm of your heartbeat. Notice the beat or sound of it. For a minute or so, you may even want to tap your hand onto your knee with each beat of your heart. This precious, powerful, sacred beat is your rhythm of life. It's so often taken for granted or not even noticed. Your rhythm of life, your heartbeat, your spirit, carries you through each day, and it is a miracle because you don't have to do anything. Just be! Your rhythm of life makes you and me a miracle. Thank your heartbeat and apologize for taking it for granted.

What happens when that rhythm of life is taken away? What happens when you die or encounter a near-death experience? I will share my journey . . . as the miracle of life lives on in another unique, sacred way.

* * *

I will never forget my first night at Dixie Regional Medical Center in St. George, Utah. I was admitted because of extreme fatigue, high fever, and difficulty breathing. I hadn't felt well for some time, but I figured I caught a virus that was going around and I would get over it before long. But I was not getting over it. It was getting the best of me. After being admitted into the hospital, my doctor ordered some tests.

When Dr. Teresa Bowers informed me I had PCP (Pneumocystic carinii Pneumonia), just hearing those three letters, I knew I was

124

facing death. PCP was the number one leading cause of death among people with AIDS. Not only was I HIV positive, I was now diagnosed with AIDS. A four letter word that holds so much power. Was I going to let those four letters take away *my* power?

My doctor told me I needed to go on strong and aggressive Western medication or I would die from PCP. Just hearing her words made my head spin. My mind was racing for answers. How could I possibly go on Western drugs when they were everything I was against? I had taught and embraced Eastern philosophy and healing since my Spiritual Guide introduced me to it when I had suffered with anorexia. How could I possibly put my faith in my doctor and Western drugs? For hours I cried, horrified and fearful. I didn't want to die, but for me I felt that if I took the medication, the toxicity of the drugs would kill me. So was I going to let PCP take my life, or was I going to let the drugs kill me? I signed a form rejecting the use of Western medications for PCP.

I lay in my hospital bed, hooked up to oxygen to help me breathe easier. Then I prayed, and prayed, and prayed. I prayed for answers, but my mind would not silence itself enough to hear. However, after several hours, I was able to still my mind and hear what needed to be done.

In a semi-meditative state, I heard, *"My child, unlike the time before when you were not to take AZT or Western medications, now you must take what your doctor offers you. Bless the medication. Take it with ease, and be conscious of what is given to you."*

I thought my mind was playing games. How could I possibly take these medications? Again silence overcame me and I heard a familiar voice from one of my Spiritual Teachers tell me, *"You must take the medicine, and as you do so, bless each and every pill you receive."*

125

I buzzed the nurse and told her I would take the medication my doctor had previously prescribed for me. I was immediately hooked up to an IV drug, and as various pills sat in my left hand, I held a glass of water in my right hand. My hands shook as I looked at the pills, and tears welled up in my eyes. I blessed each pill, yet they were the hardest things I have ever had to swallow.

I cried all night long. I felt if I fell asleep I would die. A gentle, kind, comforting nurse named Lois May visited me throughout the night. She held my hand, listened to my fears, wiped my tears, and assured me I would not die. The night was long. Endlessly long. The clock kept ticking away, and I felt like my life was too.

When my blood work came back, my doctor informed me I only had three t-cells – the white blood cells that fight infection. The average healthy person usually has 800 to 1,800 t-cells. I didn't see it as a problem though. I named my t-cells Hope, Love, and Laughter and gave them the power to make me healthy again.

Before long I overcame PCP, but shortly after that I came down with MAC/MAI (Mycobacterterium avium Complex). To me, this was far worse than anything I had ever experienced. The fatigue was severe, the diarrhea uncontrollable, the vomiting endless, the fevers extremely high, and the sweating unbearable.

For over a year, I was in and out of the hospital with MAI/ MAC. At one point I was airlifted in *Flight for Life* to Salt Lake City University Hospital where I spent three months.

The following is an account of my life during 1996 through the first three months of 1997:

My life force is weak and dim. I lie helpless in a cold, sterile hospital bed, hooked up to IVs for treatments and transfusions. Implanted in my chest is a Hickman catheter, a special device for

TPN feedings, and deep within me, a catheter is imbedded, its tubing ending in a bag to collect my urine. As I gasp for air, a nurse hooks me up to oxygen. Each breath of life is more precious and difficult to take.

I've lost my independence. I'm no longer capable of caring for myself. I buzz the nurse to adjust my skeletal body, to ease my pain.

A handful of pills, one more shot, one more IV, a familiar face exploring my body. My sheets, gown, pillow, and entire body drenched with sweat. Fevers of over 103 degrees. Then chills, cold as ice. I lie in bed and suddenly start to shake. I close my fists tightly, thinking it's an earthquake. But it isn't an earthquake, it's me, shivering. When will it end? The tubes, the suffering, the emotions, and confusion. Is death knocking at my door?

Nothing stays in my body. The stench of vomit and diarrhea envelops me and permeates my surroundings.

Why do people call? Why do they come visit me? Do they come out of curiosity or to bid their farewells? Too exhausted to return conversation, I fall into a deep sleep. Abruptly, as always, someone wakens me. Their cold hands touch my body as they take my blood pressure.

Day in and day out, endlessly the same. Am I living? I fear not. I no longer have a vital quality of life. I would much rather die than live a life in my condition. I am suffering and so is my family. I know my life is slipping away.

Many times in the past, I wanted my life to end. But I'm not ready to die yet. My heart and soul ache for my daughter, Jeaneen. I must embrace her one more time.

I remember vividly the night before my near-death experience. I was in Dixie Regional Medical Center. A loving embrace from someone familiar awakened me. Softly, I strained to say, "Dad." My vision blurred as tears filled my eyes. I looked around my bedside and recognized my sister Joyce and my mother. Mom sat close to my side, helpless in her wheelchair. She reached out, held my hand, and I could see sadness in her eyes. Tears streamed down her face as I heard her say, "We love you, honey." Then without hesitation Dad said, "Jeaneen's on her way. She's flying in tonight."

Suddenly, all my stored-up tears flooded out like a dam had been broken. I could barely talk, yet knowing Jeaneen would be by my side brought joy to my heart.

One by one Mom, Dad, and Joyce leaned over and gave me a kiss and hug. Weak but determined, I lifted my arms around them and tried to embrace them. Few words were spoken, perhaps everything had already been expressed—our deep love for one another. Due to Mom's health problems, my parents didn't stay long.

Before Jeaneen arrived, Joyce washed my face, combed my snarled hair, and put lipstick on me. I laughed inside. Joyce probably had not held a tube of lipstick in her hand in over 20 years. I could feel her love for me through the care she continued to give me.

That evening when Jeaneen walked into my hospital room, she stood by the doorway and looked at me as though I were a stranger. As I caught a glimpse of her, a surge of energy came over me. Calmness filled my soul as my heart filled with excitement to see my beloved daughter. Yet, it frightened me as she continued to stand in the doorway. As she stared at me, I realized my thin, pale, pasty body must have been a pathetic sight.

Then, within a matter of seconds, she burst into tears, dashed toward me, bent over the hospital bed, and put her arms around me. Tears streamed down our cheeks as we embraced one another.

"Mommy! I love you!"

I managed to gather what little strength I had to say, "I love you."

After regaining what little composure I could muster, Joyce said she was going back to my house for the night. Jeaneen quickly asked, "Mom, can I stay here with you all night?"

My eyes must have gleamed as I nodded, "Yes!" She lowered the bed safety rail, sat next to me, and held my hand. Softly she placed her hands on my face, looked into my eyes, and told me how much she loved and missed me. Tears of joy rolled down our faces. Jeaneen smiled as she wiped my runny nose with a tissue and then lightly rubbed away my teardrops and hers.

"Oh Mommy, I want to make you well. I want to be able to do things together again. I want to bring you home and take care of you."

I wanted to smile at her, but it felt like a knife had sliced me open and ripped my insides out. Jeaneen asked, "Mom, can I crawl into bed with you and hold you in my arms? I'll try not to move or hurt you." I welcomed her to join me. The warmth of her body next to mine and her hand and arm placed on my chest made me feel safe and loved.

"I love you!" I could feel my shoulder get moist from her tears. No words could describe the love we shared for one another. Jeaneen knew the intense love I had for her through my actions, words, support, and guidance. She also knew I loved her because of how I allowed her the freedom to express herself throughout her life. Our love also took the form of a loving look, a gentle caress, our special kiss, or holding hands as we did so often. These simple things brought me comfort.

Hours passed and we fell asleep in each other's arms. Throughout the night we didn't get much rest, though. In the morning, when breakfast arrived for Jeaneen, I could tell she was exhausted. After she ate her meal, she said, "Mom, if you don't mind, I'd like to drive back to your house and take a shower. I'll be right back. Do you want anything from home?"

I managed to find the strength to say, "Just you." I watched as she slowly walked out into the corridor.

My body trembled and I became weaker. Jeaneen had been lying by my side, but now I was awake and alone. Or should I say, I thought I was alone! All of a sudden, my Spirit lifted out of me, and it hovered over my physical body in the bed below. I immediately felt healed, more alive, and freer than I had ever felt before. Warmth of love and inner peace cascaded from within me.

After my Spirit floated over my body for a short time, two Spirit Beings, one male and one female, appeared before me. They were dressed in long white gowns. They looked as if they were physical, yet I could see through them, just like my other Spirit Guides who have been with me for so many years. The Spirit Beings reached out and took my hand. Telepathically, they told me they wanted to show me a review of my life.

In an instant, I was taken to different scenes throughout the world, and events in my lifetime with numerous people and situations. As I was above looking down and witnessing the scenes, telepathically the Spirit Beings said, *"Look at the difference you have made in their lives."* After I had seen numerous events and some people I had forgotten, and the impact I had made on so many lives, the Spirit Beings took me away.

I felt myself move into a bright Tunnel of Light. I noticed gray figures like people on each side of the tunnel trying to reach out and touch me. Swiftly, I passed unfamiliar faces that looked at me. I wanted to cry out, "Where are my brothers, Tommy and Raymond? Where are my friends and loved ones who have gone before me?" Yet, I was silent.

At what seemed to be the end of the Tunnel there appeared, once again, the most beautiful, warm, brilliant, radiant, loving light shining upon me and enveloping me. I was awed by the beauty, peace, and serenity. Telepathically, from the Light of God, I heard, *"My child, unlike the time before, you have a choice. You can come with me or you can return and continue your life."* The silent, loving telepathic voice went on to say, *"Before you make your decision, I want to show you one more thing."*

Instantaneously, I relived – not reviewed, but *relived* – my life with Jeaneen. I felt her in my womb; I felt the sensation of her first kick within me; I rubbed my tummy, sang to her, and told her how much I loved her before she was even born. Then, I relived her actual birth, felt her tiny lips suck on my breasts. I listened to her gurgles and coos. I smelled the wonderful scent of my baby from her first bath. I relived numerous experiences and special times with Jeaneen, throughout her 18 years. There was laughter, playfulness, tears, as well as the challenges we had shared together through our life journey. There were moments when we were not only mother and daughter, but friends, companions, spiritual teachers, and so much more to one another. We felt blessed to be together.

Then, a spark of Light hit me, and once again I appeared before the Light of God. Telepathically, I was asked, *"My child, what is your decision?"*

The intense love, healing, and peace I felt in the Light was so profound. Yet silently, I thought, I can't leave Jeaneen. Not yet! Telepathically I expressed in sincere love, "I have to return to my daughter."

Immediately and without warning, I was in the hospital bed. My deteriorated body still looked like a corpse. However, I was alive! Tears of joy streamed down my cheeks. For the next hour, my entire Being glowed with love and light. As I closed my eyes, I could see bursts of Light going into every cell, sparkling and vibrating with energy. The healing power of God was restoring me cell by cell. The sensation felt like effervescent bubbles. It was as if I were being newly created with life, strength, and energy. The intense surge and vibrant life force running through me was so strong, I knew before long I would be back in my Earthly home, healthy and fully alive!

I had reclaimed my life, and my entire Being glowed with love for Jeaneen and life. Silently, I prayed and gave thanks for all I experienced. Before me appeared new beginnings, dreams, fresh goals, freedom, health, serenity, inner peace, and love.

When Jeaneen arrived back at hospital, from taking a shower at my home, she noticed my life force was different. I no longer looked pale and pasty, my skin tone was back to normal, I had a sparkle in my eyes, a smile on my face, and energy to carry on a conversation. She was amazed at the miracle, and felt blessed I returned to life—for her.

A few days later in meditation, I asked why I did not see Tommy and Raymond. I was told, *"My child, if you saw the one you call Tommy your decision might have been harder."*

The next day, Tommy appeared to me as he had so many times in the past. He said, *"Sharon, you do not have to die to be with me. I am always with you and I love you."*

Before long I was back home and in the loving care and hands of Jeaneen, Joyce, my friends Jo and Brenda, my nurses Marie and Gloria, and my nurse's aide Kelly. By November 1997, I realized I had to move back to an area where I could receive the appropriate healthcare for AIDS. I knew Los Angeles, San Francisco, and San Diego had outstanding HIV/AIDS communities. However, if I moved back to Los Angeles, I would allow myself to become an active volunteer in the AIDS community, and that was not what I needed at the time. San Francisco seemed too cold for my body and bones. So I consciously chose San Diego. Even though I only knew one person there, I trusted I would be guided in all the right areas. My choice was confirmed when I heard in meditation that my new home would be in San Diego.

* * *

Now take a slow deep breath. Your breath has not become silent. Listen to it. Notice your breath of life. Notice the rhythm, the beat and sound of your precious heart. This is your rhythm of life. Do not take life for granted. Honor your life force and give homage to it. Life is sacred and so is death!

I've learned a lot from my experience with HIV/AIDS and the use of Integrative and Western medications. I now embrace the Western and Eastern ways and realize that both have great benefits. When I have to take Western drugs, I hold the medicine in my hand and say a prayer. I give thanks and bless the researchers, doctors, pharmacy staff, medicines, and the positive results that come from them. For many years, I only had my three powerful t-cells, Hope, Love and Laughter, but now I have more than I can name, which has put me out of the danger zone of an opportunistic infection. I will continue to go within and listen to my body and the wisdom I receive in my meditations. Since my near-death experience, I was able to go off the Western drugs for some time.

I'm now able to fulfill the second part of my life purpose which was given to me in 1984 – to write books.

Millions of people throughout the world have had near-death experiences, but you don't have to be at the threshold of death to receive the lessons.

Sacred Living, Sacred Dying is a gift of tools which will allow you to *"Practice Dying."* This can lead to embracing people, events, circumstances, and all that life and death hold with greater compassion, love, and understanding.

Just for a moment, ask yourself these questions: If I were to die tomorrow, would I feel complete and at peace? Have I told those who are important in my life how much I love and appreciate them? Is there any situation where I'm holding back from speaking my truth? Now is the time to be all you can be. There's no other time but NOW. Share your wisdom, your gifts, and your life journey with your loved ones, so your memories will forever live on in their hearts and minds.

Whether you are in optimum health or ill, no one knows when his or her last breath of life might occur. After reading *Sacred Living, Sacred Dying: A Guide to Embracing Life and Death* and my near-death experience, I hope you'll enjoy taking the time to share your *Legacy of Love* through the story of your life and create a unique memorial or celebration which truly represents you. By doing so, your friends and loved ones can pay a personal tribute to you and you can remember them in a special way as well.

I wish I had given my family and friends a *Sacred Planner* before I faced my death. I know it would have been a thoughtful and sacred gift to give. Since my near-death experience, I've had the opportunity to prepare and honor my loved ones with my *Sacred Planner*. I know in my heart all my wishes will be carried out "My Way" (as Frank Sinatra crooned,) and I will die in dignity, as memories of me and my legacy of love live on.

I want to congratulate you on embracing the sacredness of life and death, and for searching your heart and memory for meaningful words, things, and precious memories that your friends and loved ones will cherish forever.

I know the saying, *"Peace of Mind is Priceless"* is a cliché, however, the *Sacred Planner* you leave your loved ones will bring priceless peace of mind to all.

I honor and bless your life and spirit. I also honor and bless your transition. May every soul and spirit be honored in a sacred way which truly represents their life journey.

Love and Blessings,

Sharon Lund

If you would like to contact me for speaking engagements, book signings, workshops, presentations, or for any other reason, please visit my website at www.sharonlund.com. I would love to hear from you.

You can also purchase *Sacred Living, Sacred Dying – The Workbook* on my website.

Acknowledgments

❧   ❧

Acknowledgments

With Deepest Appreciation

Infinite Sprit, God, thank you for showing me your brilliant, radiant, loving light and eternal love. *Sacred Living, Sacred Dying: A Guide to Embracing Life and Death* would not have come about had I not had my near-death experience. I feel honored and blessed to embrace the sacredness of dying and death, and for reminding me there's no separation.

My beautiful, loving Jeaneen, I love you so much and I'm blessed to be able to continue to share life experiences with you. Thank you for being my strength when I was weak. In the center of my heart and mind I cherish the loving connection we have with one another. You are my gift from God.

It's with great honor and respect that I send love and blessings to my past and present Spirit Guides and Angels who have helped to orchestrate my life journey in a Divine way.

Dad and Mom (Tom and Jean – Mom now in Spirit), Jeaneen, my sister Joyce, Brenda Butler and Jo Jones, Lois and Brooks Baker, George Stoddard, the staff and volunteers of *Southern Utah AIDS Task Force*, Rev. Steve and Jean Keplinger, Lois Dietrich and Steven Lowe, you saw me through my darkest hours and I can't begin to tell you how important your gentle touch, your loving words, your every lasting support, your silence and understanding, and your prayers meant to me. God has truly blessed me with your everlasting friendship and love.

Hector thank you for your constant support, understanding, and patience. Side-by-side you have been with my as I continue my life purpose. Only you and I know how much you have contributed to my life. You are truly a gifted healer and I feel blessed God brought you into my life.

To my Circle of Friends throughout the world who prayed for me during my trying times, God bless you and thank you for keeping me in your thoughts and prayers. Your prayers were answered.

To my entire medical team in Southern Utah, Southern California, and Africa, thank you for your expertise and for treating me as a family member.

My Wonderful Supporters

I want to lovingly thank the following people for endorsing *Sacred Living, Sacred Dying: A Guide to Embracing Life and Death:*

Stephen and Ondrea Levine, you have awakened and inspired the lives of millions of people, and I've grown and learned so much from your workshops, seminars, books, and our personal experiences throughout the decades. The valuable knowledge I've gained from you I will embrace forever and share with humanity, as I continue to *"Practice Dying."* I feel blessed and honored to have received your gracious words in my Foreword. Stephen, you are truly a gifted teacher, and I feel fortunate I have personally been able to learn from you. Ondrea and Stephen, I continue to send you love and blessings. Namasté.

Joan Borysenko, Ph.D., thank you for your vast wealth of information and for bringing forth the spiritual side in such an elegant way. You are one of the few leaders and role models for women today, and I feel honored to have learned so much from you.

Dr. John Demartini, through your teachings and instructions I have been given a clear vision of my full potential. Thank you for your gift of wisdom and for embracing my vision. I support you in your goal of sharing your wisdom and insights with at least three billion people.

Christian Richard Demlow, DMin BCC, when I'm with you, your soft spoken words of love and truth brings a sense of inner peace to my soul. I'm honored to have worked with you and call you my friend.

Ken Druck, Ph. D. and Jack E. Stephens, J.D., LL.M. I prayed to God and you appeared. Thank you for your new friendship, support, and for believing in all I do. I look forward to working with you as we embrace the gifts we share with others.

Greg Hahn, R.N., your warm, gentle, loving words and support show the great compassion and understanding you have. How fortunate for the men, women, and children you assist who are terminally ill, and people like me, who know you as a long-time friend.

Bernie Siegel, M.D., you too have inspired the lives of millions of people throughout the world through your teachings, wisdom, and presence. Your inspirational words hold a special place in my heart. I deeply respect and appreciate your compassion, love, and understanding and for helping me embody the truth. Thank you also for sharing with me the sacredness of your near-death. We've been blessed with this beautiful gift we have experienced. I understand how hard it was to return after having been in the light and love of God, and to leave the sacred feeling of complete love, peace, and perfect health. However, I'm thankful you and I returned to continue our life's purpose.

Contributors

There are several people I want to acknowledge and show my appreciation to for taking time out of their busy work schedule to review various sections of my book. Doug and Claudia Kimball and Leslie Martin at *Controversial Bookstore;* Doug Flaker, Mortuary Family Service Counselor; Arron Grimes at *Wade Funeral Home;* Attorney Arthur Chettle; Lisa Stocks at *Lifesharing Community Organ & Tissue Donation;* the staff at *Fort Rosecrans National Cemetery;* Barbara Callahan at the *Naval Medical Center* in San Diego; Billy and Kimberley Campbell at *Ramsey Creek;* Jerrigrace Lyons at *Final Passages;* Barbara Kernan and Eric Putt at *Thresholds;* Don Brawley and George Frankel at *Eternal Reefs.* Thank you for the expertise and knowledge in your work field and all the important information you shared with me and the readers. Your contribution has made a profound difference in my book.

My Supportive Book Team

Monica Hagen thank you for sharing your gift of editing, on this journey called *Sacred Living, Sacred Dying.*

Jeaneen Lund, not only are you my beautiful, loving daughter, you are an extremely gifted, talented, and versatile photographer with a keen eye for uniqueness and creativity. Thank you for capturing the essence of me.

Jan Phillips, you focus the lens on beauty and truth and I feel honored to have one of your exquisite photos on the cover of *Sacred Living, Sacred Dying.*

Miko Radcliffe your talent as a graphic design artist shines brightly on the cover of this book, and in all that we have shared.

Appendix

Bible Scriptures – Samples

It's important to remember every translation of the Bible has different nuances in wording, so if you choose to have scriptures read, use the wording from a Bible that makes you feel comfortable.

Bible Scriptures that Convey the Symbolism of White Doves

GENESIS

8:8-12   Noah releases a dove to see if the flood had receded, and it returns with an olive branch.

PSALMS

55:6   And I said, Oh that I had wings like a dove! Then would I fly away and be at rest.

MATTHEW

3:16-17   When John baptizes Jesus, the spirit of God descended upon him like a dove.

Other Bible Scriptures Often Read at Memorials

PSALMS

23:1-4   The Lord is my shepherd.

23:6   Dwell in the House of the Lord forever.

130   Assurance of the Lord's forgiveness.

ECCLESIASTES

3:1-8   Time for everything.

ISAIAH

57:1-2   Those who walk uprightly enter into peace. They find rest as they lie in death.

65:17-25   New Heavens and a New Earth.

LAMENTATIONS

3:25   The Lord is good to him who waits for him, to the soul that seeks him.

3:32-33   The Lord's unfailing love and compassion.

MATTHEW

5:1-5   Jesus gives the sermon on the mount.

6:9-15   Jesus teaches about prayer. The Lord's Prayer.

6:19-21   Treasure in heaven.

MARK

15:33-39   Jesus dies on the cross.

16:1-6   Jesus rises from the dead.

JOHN

3:16   For God so loved the world that he gave his only Son.

5:24-27   The dead will hear the voice of the Son of God; and those who hear it will live.

6:35-40   Jesus is the True Bread of Life.

11:25-26   Jesus is the resurrection and the life. He who believes.

14:1-6   Jesus is the way to the Father.

ROMANS

8:38-39 Nothing can separate us from God in Christ Jesus.

14:7-9 If we live, we live to the Lord: and if we die, we die to the Lord.

1 CORINTHIANS

2:9 What God has prepared for those who love him.

13:4-8 What Love is.

15:20-23 The resurrection of the dead.

2 CORINTHIANS

1:3-5 God comforts us.

1 THESSALONIANS

4:13-18 The Coming of the Lord – Do not grieve.

1 PETER

3:8-22 Live in harmony with one another.

REVELATION

21:1-7 God is making everything new.

Poems for Releasing
Your Spirit

The following are two poems which you have permission to use, if you choose, for releasing your spirit. These poems are courtesy of Rev. Art Casale, *Two Doves Ministry* in San Diego, California.

Rev. Casale's website is www.sandiegoweddingminister.com.

Flight of the Spirit

Author Unknown

The first dove released
Symbolizes the spirit and freedom of our loved one (Name).
As soul he/she wings his/her way upward
To fly in spirit on the final journey home.

The next 10 doves released
Symbolize an assembly of Angels
Guiding (Name) home.

The second set of 10 doves represents
(Name's) family and friends, whom he/she loves,
Soaring in spirit with him/her.

For all that matters in this world of ours;
What we need on this earth to fill our hours,
Is to accept a pure and simple love,
Which is sent on the wings of a dove.

Flight of the Spirit

Author Unknown

The white dove released symbolizes the
Spirit and freedom of our loved one, (Name).
As he/she flies his/her way upward to
Soar in Spirit on his/her final journey home.

As this bird finds its way home,
So does the spirit in passing,
For God will not abandon us,
But lead us home.

A Checklist for Your Loved Ones

A Checklist for Your Loved Ones.

When you die, there's a long, bewildering list of things that must be gathered or completed. Below is a checklist for your friends and loved ones. Once you've completed your *Sacred Planner*, a lot of the information your loved ones will need is included in your Planner.

This informative and helpful checklist is from the wonderful, supportive staff at *Glen Abbey Memorial Park and Mortuary* in Bonita, California.

Collection of Legal Documents:

Will
Birth certificate
Social Security number
Marriage license
Citizenship papers
Insurance policies
Bank books

Deeds to property
Auto ownership
Income tax returns
Veteran's discharge papers
Disability claims
Cemetery deed

People to Notify:

Doctors and dentist
Attorney
Employer
Insurance agent
Clubs, unions, and
    organizations

Funeral director
Cemetery official creditors
Employers of relatives not
    going to work
Clergyman
Banker

Bills to Pay:

Clergy
Clothing
Transportation
Telephone
Food
Doctors
Nurses

Hospital
Ambulance
Medical/medications
Burial estate
Funeral director
Memorial marker
Police escort (if required)

Personal Data of Deceased:

Grade school attended
High school attended
College attended
Degrees
Public, civic, religious
    offices, or positions held

Military record
Citations
Hobbies and interests
Special accomplishments
Charitable and special wishes

Future Plans:

Income
Credit
Emotional adjustment

Family adjustment
Re-budget for spousal income
    loss

Things to Remember

To save time and avoid inconvenience, we (the mortuary or funeral home) suggest that you (the survivor) bring the following information with you to the mortuary or funeral home at the time of your appointment, regarding the deceased:

1. Clothing, including undergarments.

2. Eyeglasses and jewelry – These items may remain with your loved one or be removed and returned after the service.

3. One recent photograph for cosmetic purposes.

4. Veteran's discharge papers.

5. Social Security number.

6. Life insurance policies.

7. List of 6 to 8 Pallbearers, if applicable.

8. A collection of valued photographs to illustrate your loved one's life through an Everlasting Memorial Internet archive and a multimedia scrapbook for family memories.

To facilitate death certificate requirements and placement of the newspaper notice (obituary), please provide the following information:

1. Mother's full name (including maiden name).

2. Father's full name.

3. Birthplace.

4. Education.

5. Work history.

6. Church affiliation.

7. Organizations or memberships.

8. Special achievements.

9. Names of surviving relatives and the cities in which they live (include parents, spouses, siblings, children, grand-children, grandparents, etc.)

The mortuary or funeral home can assist you with details including:

1. Date and time of the service.

2. Coordination of services with the cemetery, crematory, and airline if necessary.

3. Family transportation.

4. Monument and inscription services, where available.

5. Flowers to complement the color of the casket and clothing.

6. Everlasting Memorial Internet archive.

7. Newspaper notices/obituaries.

8. Filing the Death Certificate and ordering certified copies of the Death Certificate.

The mortuary or funeral home staff will also assist you in filing for:

1. VA benefits.

2. Social Security benefits.

3. Life insurance benefits.

LaVergne, TN USA
04 November 2009

162939LV00003B/4/P